BETWEEN TWO BREATHS

THOM MILLER
WITH VALERI MILLS BARNES

This is a non-fiction work. Names, characters, organizations, places, events, and incidents are the products of the author's memory as well as interviews conducted with others involved in the events.

Between Two Breaths

This book represents the personal views and opinions of the author and does not necessarily reflect the positions or opinions of any organization, institution, or individual with which the author is affiliated. The content presented herein is based on the author's perspective and interpretation of the subject matter. Neither the publisher nor any associated parties shall be held responsible for any consequences arising from the opinions or interpretations expressed within this book.

First paperback edition November 2025
Cover Design by: Kay McConnaughey
Interior Design: Carolyn Rafferty
Published by Berry Powell Press
Glendora, California
www.berrypowellpress.com
ISBN: 978-1-957321-26-4 (Paperback)

Praise for *Between Two Breaths*

An incredible must-read story! Thom Miller's story will move you to happy tears. His life-changing event defied nature and medicine—affecting everyone who loves him. Thom's story is a profound testament to faith, to God's presence in our darkest moments, and to a family that refuses to let go. His journey proves the human spirit, fortified by love and faith, is capable of the extraordinary. Thom's story left me feeling connected to something larger—to all that is, was, and ever will be. His story reminds us to be present for those we love and never give up on each other. A feel-good story, and a gift—proof that miracles still happen, that love transcends death, and that faith can move mountains.

—Janet Boydell, author of *Deadly Exploits*

The story, *Between Two Breaths*, tells it all: the personal experiences of a man, author Thom Miller, who drowned, was declared dead, and then brought back to life. And much of it in graphic and riveting detail. Once in my hands, I could not put it down. I believe the reader, whoever he or she may be, will have the same response. Personal experiences are probably the most compelling form of persuasion. This book is no exception. His chances of a full recovery were, as one doctor later stated, one in a thousand, and are all told in fascinating detail. The family, waiting with bated breath for answers from the hospital staff about their husband, father, and friend, draws the reader into another world where suspense reigns and every piece of good news is met with thanksgiving. But then there is also the larger story of Thom's search for meaning: the meaning of this event set into the context of his entire life. It is the story of *eternity* breaking into *time*. This broadens the story and gives it a universal meaning. God's providence in his life. Why should he have survived when other drowning victims did not? And what had happened in those twenty-two minutes that he was declared dead? He had experienced *eternity*. One can accept or question experiences, but one cannot deny them. This book contains the remarkable and unique experiences of one man. But his experiences inform every one of us.

—Abraham Friesen, Ph.D., Professor of History Emeritus,
UC Santa Barbara, Author of
Caught Between Christ and Christendom

Between Two Breaths is a true story of mostly family members rafting the whitewater of the Kings River in Central California. When author Thom Miller drowns, his near-death experience and subsequent accounts will keep you holding the edge of the next page. Thom Miller teaming up with Valeri Mills Barnes to write Thom's story was a brilliant move! Both actual wordsmiths in their own right produced a fabulous book. A page turner, *Between Two Breaths*, will not let you put it down. The narrative will keep you focused just as if you were standing in the middle of the story. For example, you'll be gasping for air and looking for a warm blanket as the account carries you downstream. Keeping the reader firmly in the center of the story is a gift and will comfortably guide you through a fascinating read.

—Ron Hughart, Author of *Beyond the Dust Bowl*
and *The Place Beyond the Dust Bowl*

Compelling and immersive! Thom Miller's profound memoir—*Between Two Breaths*—thrills the soul, shining a bright light on the power of guardian angels and how God's love and goodness surround us continuously. Miller skillfully renders a riveting account of his adventurous life, where he narrowly and inexplicably escaped death multiple times. Then, he drowned. With no pulse, no heartbeat, no breath, Miller was clinically dead for more than twenty-two minutes. Miracle after miracle brought him back to life, and to his doctor's astonishment, he suffered no brain damage. Keep the tissue box handy and prepare to be awestruck by what he experienced during his death and the role his amazing family played in his survival and recovery. Accompany Thom on this journey into heaven, where his *faith* is transformed into absolute *knowing*, and you will be richly blessed.

—Sherry Maysonave, Bestselling author of *Tatae's Promise;* IIBA Author of the Year 2025, Historical Fiction.

The memoir, *Between Two Breaths,* by Thom Miller with Valeri Mills Barnes, is a remarkable tale of one man's journey, told not only from his point of view but also from the perspectives of witnesses, eliciting authenticity and trust. Exciting from beginning to end, it's definitely worth the read.

—Marilyn Meredith, author of the *Deputy Tempe Crabtree* mystery series and the *Rocky Bluff P.D.* series.

Between Two Breaths is a wonderful read. It is intense at times, but also joyful. The author has a way of drawing you and making you feel as if you are right there with him while it is happening. This is strongest in chapter six, but is evident on every page of the book. For me, personally, it carried some emotional weight as well, since the areas and places described are right in my "back yard" where I grew up—especially when he talks about the Kings River. I highly recommend this book to anyone looking for biographical non-fiction. While it is written by a Christian, with his faith gracefully evident throughout. I believe non-Christians would enjoy it as well.

—Dave Peterson, Pastor, Loma Rica Baptist Church

Between Two Breaths is a great read. The reader will hear Thom Miller's voice as they experience the vivid action, historical "like being there" flashbacks to war-torn Vietnam, an entrepreneur's drive, and caring humanity—a greater reality than what we think. But one of the most beautiful aspects of the book is that it answers humanity's nagging question, "Why am I alive?" This is Miller's angst, which culminates in an emotional, spiritual experience with what I would call "the ancestors," those who have gone before. It is in this experience that Miller's purpose, and I would argue "our" purpose, is beautifully manifested. Between Two Breaths is a good book worth experiencing.

—Rev. Bryan Lee Martin, D.Min., author of *The Home Model*

Contents

Dedication

This book is dedicated to all seven of my children, Thomas, Timothy, Patrick, Nathan, Michael, Elizabeth, and Gregory, who were relentless in their efforts to bring me back to life and health.

Acknowledgments

I want to acknowledge the loving and generous individuals who supported me throughout the writing of this book, as well as those who assisted me during and after the events depicted in its pages. I cannot list all of them here, but love and thanks to:

First, a very long prayer chain of friends, relatives, church members, and family members—stretching all around the world—who often prayed for me and still do.

Kelly Chamberlin Miller – my wife since 1970, whose partnership has been the highlight of my life. She bore and nurtured our amazing children, with a little help from me, of course, but with her firm guidance and moral compass, we have developed as a strong family. The love we share is reflected in our children and demonstrated in this book. Her love and companionship have unbelievably blessed me.

My seven children – all of whom were constantly involved and there for Kelly and me whenever needed. I especially thank my children for their participation in the book via their voices. They were with me when these events unfolded, and they cared for me afterward. They brought much joy into my life, including their beautiful children.

My whole family – comprising nine siblings, their spouses, and their progeny, as well as my in-laws.

My mother, Loretta Miller – who passed in 2010, helped maintain the hospital vigil and insisted that the staff feed me Ambrotose while I was unconscious.

My mother-in-law, June Chamberlin – who passed in 2025, gave me unceasing encouragement and strength.

The staff and management of Kings River Expeditions – they were selfless in their efforts to assist my family and me during our time of tragedy. And the many other rafters who helped in so many ways and who were praying constantly for me.

UMC – The amazing staff at University Medical Center's (now Community Regional Medical Center) Intensive Care Unit applied their medical skills vigorously.

CHP Staff – The California Highway Patrol's helicopter pilot, Paul Dwyer, and EMT Andrea Brown, who will forever be part of my extended family.

And last but not least, Berry Powell Press and my co-writer and editor, Valeri Mills Barnes, whose relentless diligence helped turn this story into a readable book! Her skillful insights brought many diverse events into focus, which would not have made sense to a reader without her first massaging them.

Introduction

As I began writing this book, I sensed that there were aspects of my life that my readers would benefit from knowing, as they bear on my overall journey. This story is true, and I have diligently avoided exaggerations that might lead the reader to believe I have fabricated any part of it. However, over the past seven decades, events have graphically demonstrated that I was not—and am not—alone in every sense of the word, especially spiritually.

I am a believer in Jesus Christ, above all else. Growing up in Exeter, California, I had a wonderful childhood in a great family. I was an ardent Boy Scout and enjoyed the principles espoused in Scouting: the twelve points of the Scout Law, the Scout motto, and other teachings. I have never left a campsite in worse shape than I found it! In high school, I was a boarder at Bellarmine College Preparatory in San Jose—a rather exclusive school with high academic standards. My education was thorough and life-changing. Since boarders made up about a fifth of the student body and lived in campus dorms, we grew pretty close to one another. We boarders came to Bellarmine from all over the world, with unique backgrounds, and we formed friendships that have lasted a lifetime.

When my father died suddenly in 1983, while appearing to be in excellent health, I was dumbfounded. He was sixty-five, and I began to question my mortality. I often wondered if I would even live as long as he did. My odds were not good with my wild motorcycle experiences and other reckless behaviors. I had a perplexing premonition, which was repeated several times in the late 1990s and early 2000s, that I would die before the age of sixty. Nothing was written anywhere to substantiate that feeling, but the thought recurred often, and I would put it out of my mind.

I practiced some behavior modification, but not in deference to that hunch. As the father of seven exceptional children and a very talented and loving wife, I needed to be in the moment for them, so that's where I kept my whole focus. This suspicion didn't really affect my daily life, but it was felt, and I grew to accept it.

I have had many harrowing experiences in my life in which I could or should have died. Most of my friends know of these events and often say I must be a cat with nine lives, but nine is an understatement.

I want to make the point that God blesses us according to His will, not what we do or how good or bad we are—you cannot earn special treatment. But I've found, in my case, that there are many examples of His love for me; His care is demonstrated through the intercession of guardian angels. It has been graphic, sometimes subtle, occasionally like a head slap, and often like a gentle nudge, but always unmistakable, reinforcing my faith. I call it a broad blessing.

That is to say that I'm not surprised that the experience presented in this book turned out the way it did. It was in keeping with God's tacit promise to love and care for me, displayed in a record of events that amaze me.

Note: For authenticity's sake, I will not be the only one telling the stories and narrating this book. Because I wasn't "present" for specific periods in the story, my children, my wife, and my brother, who witnessed the event I'm sharing here, will add their perspectives on what happened. I'm grateful to them for being my eyes, ears, and voice when I could not fend for myself.

Prologue

It must be midnight, maybe later. Too quiet. Subdued lighting. What's going on?

I'm awake, lying on my back, looking at the ceiling. *Why can't I move?* I can't control any part of my body, not even my head, so I can't look for a wall clock to check the time. *Is anybody here?* I don't hear anyone moving about.

I recognize the sounds of a respirator, a blood pressure monitor, and other equipment I can't identify.

Wait a minute! I must be in the hospital! This is not my bed!

While studying pre-med at College of the Sequoias in Visalia, I worked at Kaweah Delta Hospital, often doing night shifts. I recognize the quiet and the background sounds of medical equipment whirring and the ventilation system humming. *This is definitely a hospital!*

I have tubes down my throat. *The ventilator is controlling my breathing! I'm helpless! I can't talk; I can't get anyone's attention. Is there anyone here?*

Dealing with whatever this is, but having no memory of where I am and how I got here, is troubling me. The tube in my mouth and throat won't let me move my lips. It is all so strange.

Why isn't anyone passing by and checking in on me? Is there no one here but me?

It's so hushed and ominous; the absence of life is alarming.

What happened? Did I go on a serious drinking binge, pass out somewhere, and someone brought me here as a lesson in behavior management? This is so bizarre. I can't move my hands, fingers, or toes. I can't detect if they are still there, as I feel nothing. I have no sense of smell. However, what's worse is forgetting everything.

I'm lying here, trying to remember what might have happened. Suddenly, I see a vision developing on the ceiling. I think it's a vision, as that's the only word that comes to mind. It's like watching television—a Technicolor movie playing on the ceiling tiles. It is vibrant, bright, silent, and sinister. The ominous feeling comes from within, like I have a good reason to be afraid. Still, the scene is beautiful and exciting.

The colors of the water, rocks, and trees in this apparition are the most vibrant I've ever seen. As I watch, I begin to discern that I am looking down at a rapidly rushing river from maybe thirty feet above. There are some major whitewater rapids below. Near a large rock at the river's edge, I can see a churning "keeper"—where the rock forces the surging water down, and as it hits the rock, it flows up, then down again. And I can see the keeper pulling water down and, moments later, pushing it to the surface repeatedly. This happened several times as I watched in wonder.

Staring at this beautiful and powerful scene, I now remember something that might explain all this. This afternoon, my boys and I left for a whitewater rafting trip on the upper Kings River. But the last thing I remember is driving east into the mountains toward Pine Flat Lake with three of my sons. Were we in an accident on the way?

I watch the beauty of the churning river on the ceiling, and then, just as suddenly as the vision appeared, it grays out and disappears.

My heart is pounding, and my mind is racing now. What has happened since we left for the river? *Am I dead? How did I end up here and in this bed? Where are my boys? What if...? Okay, Thom, stop. Don't go there. Pull yourself together.*

I'm praying for answers.

Chapter 1
WHO'S PAYING FOR THIS?
February 3, 2006

"Hey, Dad, I've heard good things about a whitewater rafting company on the Kings River. How about we plan a family junket?" It was late afternoon, and my oldest son, Thomas, was on the other end of the line.

"Sounds crazy! I've never done anything like that before, but it might be fun. Do you think all the brothers could do it? What kind of equipment would we need?" I have six sons and one daughter. The boys began calling themselves "the brothers" many years ago. It stuck, and it's a common phrase for us even today.

"It's easy. They provide all the rafting stuff, including wetsuits, and a place to park the cars. We show up, and it's like a campout for two days. There's a big bonfire at night after dinner; all we need are sleeping bags! They have a great track record, so if you want to, check them out."

"Okay, I'll do that," I said. This idea appealed to me.

"I think I told you, but remember, Dad, Mike, and I went on a rafting trip last year, or maybe two years ago," Thomas said. "We were like, man, this is something we should do with the brothers and Dad. So let's do it!"

I wasn't surprised when Thomas called me that day, in early February 2006, and proposed another adventure. My family is very close-knit. The boys are all between six feet five and six feet eight. Elizabeth, however, is five feet eight, like her mom. They're all athletic and enjoy sports.

"I like it!" I said. "Set it up, and we'll find out who else wants to go. Once we confirm the number of rafters, you can call the rafting company to reserve seats for us. Since I'm a member, I'll check out their record at the Better Business Bureau."

I worked a lot when my kids were growing up, but I made an effort to maintain a balance. My days as CEO of Bullard Uniforms were relatively uncomplicated. Our main store was located in Fresno, but we also had three additional stores in Sacramento, Dublin, and Santa Barbara. Most of the time, I was on my own schedule, allowing me some slack time. My wife was, and is, a people person, so she handled customer interactions and inventory management, while I dealt with administrative tasks. This gave me time to do things with my kids, like hiking in the Sierras or skiing with them, which we didn't do as often as I would have liked. However, we were always busy doing something, even around the house—playing basketball or volleyball, which they all enjoyed and excelled at.

I'd always regretted not getting them into Boy Scouts because I found it very useful as I was growing up. The disciplines, the skillsets, the adventures—some of the things I learned from my father, who had been a Scoutmaster in Exeter when I was a kid, are with me today.

We supported their desire to be lifeguards at Wild Water Adventures, a large and popular water park east of town. It was something they all tried out for and did every summer. They became great swimmers and developed a deep respect for the water, even though it was just a summer job. Tough job for teenage boys, watching girls in bathing suits all day, and even doing the occasional rescue.

Our city, Fresno, is situated in the heart of California's Central San Joaquin Valley, the world's agricultural heartland. Every kind of produce and fruit is grown all around us. Summers can sometimes reach temperatures of over a hundred and ten degrees, making water parks a wonderful place. Whole families are welcome to come and bring picnic baskets to enjoy lunch and dinner on site. The lifeguards have to be responsible enough to maintain peace and security, and through example, demonstrate respect for authority, something my boys learned at home anyway. However, I liked it reinforced when they worked as lifeguards.

The day after Thomas presented the brilliant idea of going rafting, I called Susan at the BBB (Better Business Bureau) and was pleasantly surprised by how quickly she could fill me in.

"Hello, Mr. Miller. Give me a moment, and I'll give you a rundown." Only five minutes later, she was back on the line. "They have been in business for thirty-three years and have never had a casualty or any accidents. Their customers have nothing but good things to say about them. You'll have a great time!"

"Susan, you folks are great. I appreciate your help."

I called Thomas when I got home, and he already had firm commitments from his siblings, Patrick, Nathan, Michael, and Greg.

"Dad, I talked to Tim, but he said, 'I have a bum knee from a basketball accident, so I'm out, but I'll be there in spirit.'" That was a bit disappointing to hear, but I fully understood.

"We'll need to get up there on Thursday night because they start bright and early on Friday," Thomas said. "Based on the snowfall this winter, the snowmelt should be in full swing at the end of May—makes for swift water!"

"Class 3, you think?" I asked.

"Most of it is considered Class 3, but who knows. We can handle it!" Class three rapids are somewhat challenging and require technical skill and savvy maneuvering.

"Yeah, you airborne guys always say that!" I said. Thomas had been an airborne medic in the Army. "It depends entirely on the weather and how much snowmelt is happening, right? I hope it's warm for spring. Can't wait!"

When I talked to Michael about an hour later, he said, "Dad, Thomas and I have rafted for the last three years. We always took the front of the boat, which is the most active part of the rafting team. Whenever you hit a rapid, that's the guys in the front. They have to drag the rest of the boat over the rapids. So, you'll probably sit in the back because of your bad shoulder."

"No problem, then!" I was not going to miss this.

"Well, it was a lot of fun. And though we've seen boats go over, we've never experienced it. Still, when it happens, it's not a big deal."

"Great! I'm looking forward to it!" I began planning what to pack. As a diabetic, I added my insulin kit to the list in my head.

Thomas, an exceptional organizer, called several of his friends and invited them, as well as my brother Gordon, whom we call Gordie. Gordie had no conflicts with the date—he had asked his son Jeremy to go too. Thomas's friend, Nick French, a basketball star from nearby Clovis West High, was also available. We lived in Central's school district back then, and Clovis West was a perennial adversary, giving us much fodder for teasing one another.

Patrick called me not long after Michael. He said, "We all wanted some buddies, too, you know? Along with Nick French, we also added Drew Zachmeyer and Ben Martin." This trip would be a party—the kind of thing I'd been telling my kids about since my Boy Scout camping days. It was starting to take shape as a serious adventure. Thomas texted that KRE (Kings River Expeditions) would reserve space for us for May 26-27, with river trips on both days. All meals would be provided by their staff.

The Kings River is the central attraction of Kings Canyon National Park. Over the eons, it has cut a cavernous canyon out of the granite mountain that features Kings Canyon. It is second in depth behind the Grand Canyon. Along the rim is Highway 180, which goes from Fresno to the end of the road in the National Park at Cedar Grove. Along the edge of the highway are cutouts where you can pull over and look into the gorge, offering a frightening view.

Every year, the snowmelt in the Sierra Nevada mountain range flows into rivers that empty into the Central Valley, also known as the San Joaquin Valley. It used to feed into Tulare Lake, a formerly large freshwater lake in the valley basin. It was the largest freshwater lake west of the Mississippi. The wind in the Valley regularly came from the north; since the lake was shallow, the northern and southern banks moved many miles each day as the wind shifted them. Dense growths of tules, an indigenous bulrush with tall reeds like bamboo, surrounded the lake. The Yokuts, comprising many small "tribelets," lived among the tules, building large rafts with the plant so that their entire villages could move with the changing banks and the wind. Since they were short, with an average height of about five feet, they could escape their enemies by dispersing into the tules, which grew to over six feet high.

In 1954, the Kings River was dammed, as were the Kern and San Joaquin Rivers, and the Tulare Lake rapidly disappeared, leaving thousands of acres of what is now fertile farmland. The lake that formed behind the Kings River dam is Pine Flat Lake, which now catches the snowmelt and prevents the flooding that used to occur. The Kings, Kern, and San Joaquin rivers trickle into the marsh near Stockton, eventually draining into the San Francisco Bay.

Heading east from Fresno on Highway 180 is a scenic and easy drive. The turnoff to Pine Flat is just past Centerville, a tiny settlement near the dam's base. That turnoff leads to a road that follows the north edge of Pine Flat Lake, eventually coming to the river where it parallels its north bank for several miles. It's a narrow, winding road and requires slow driving. Several miles on that road takes you to Dinky Creek Crossing, a wooden bridge over the Kings. You can cross the river there or continue along the road. Crossing over, though, brings you to a flat area where you can camp, and where KRE had staked out their base camp.

I had often taken my family up the river in late summer because the water was very low and slow, making it friendly for the kids to float on air mattresses. Huge crawdads lived in many of the pools along the river, so we'd invariably come home with the makings of some great gumbo.

Michael called again later in the evening and explained why he wanted to get us together for this trip.

"We were all fish, growing up!" Michael laughed. "You know, we're all good swimmers—weren't some of us swimming before we were walking? Remember Grandma June saying she thought her kids were seeing who could get rid of their children the fastest because they constantly dropped us off at the water park?"

"Yep! And she was telling the truth!" I said. "She said we all found out that sending all the kids to the water park for the summer was cheaper than paying for childcare." She wasn't wrong.

"Yeah, so the older cousins would watch out for the younger cousins," Michael said. "Some of us were still in diapers and going to the water park. So I think some of us might have learned to walk and swim simultaneously."

He was right. Some of them did just that. My boys were excellent swimmers.

Once I heard Gordie was coming with us, I called him. "Hey, are you ready for this? I've never rafted on rapids, have you? But I have no doubt we can pull it off."

"No, I've never rafted, but I had merit badges in rowing, canoeing, and lifesaving," Gordie said. "And I worked at the waterfront at the Boy Scout camp. So, I mean, I love river stuff, and I think it will be fun. You were already gone from home when I was active in the Boy Scouts—until I was seventeen. Besides, Dad instilled all that in us, right? Did you know I also spent three years as a camp staffer at Camp Miramichi at Huntington Lake, where I taught merit badges in lifesaving, rowing, and small-boat sailing. Oh, even motor boating!"

"Yeah, I missed a lot of that part of your life. And yep, Dad took the lead, didn't he? I'm glad you're going with us, Gordie! We'll have some bro time too!"

I had never rafted either. The closest I came to it was floating on air mattresses in a ditch in the summer.

Living most of my life in an agricultural part of Tulare County, I was accustomed to seeing shallow ditches in the fields that distribute fast-moving water. It was mainly healthy, well water, which was pretty clean, or had come from the river. It was being distributed to the fields where vegetables were being grown.

To control the flow, there are occasional "dams" in the ditches—weirs, we called them—and the water would flow over the weir and continue. Where it crashed over the weir, there was a surging flow of water on the other side, moving the water up and down and in a curling motion, creating what looked like rolling in the water's surface. I had never found it ominous or frightening, but they are interesting to watch.

Several of my friends and I were floating on air mattresses in a ditch one hot summer day, one of our favorite ways to beat the heat. When we got to a weir, we got out, walked around it, and planned to jump back in on the other side. However, one friend went straight into this bobbing water, which we were later told is called a "keeper." As I watched him enter it, I thought, "No big deal. He can swim out of it."

I was shocked when it became evident it was overcoming him, and as we watched, it seemed to worsen. He frantically tried to escape by surging downstream, but he couldn't get out of it.

One guy realized what was happening and waded downstream, then jumped in and grabbed him from the other side of the keeper. We didn't know it, but he had swallowed water and had run out of breath. It had never occurred to me that an innocuous air mattress floating down an irrigation ditch could be deadly.

Now, planning this trip, while I recalled that incident, my brother and I were reasonably confident in our feelings that we were athletic and strong enough to handle the Kings River, and we would love every minute of it.

A few days before the May 25th trip, I called Nathan. "Are you guys all ready for this thing?"

"You bet your sweet bippy, baby! We're here at my house doing strategy. Are you coming over?"

"I'll be there in five." Nothing could have kept me away.

Nathan and Thomas had purchased Granville homes on Sycamore, a fairly new development in west Fresno. But it used to be a one-hundred-acre fig orchard where I would run before Granville turned it into houses three years earlier. It was three minutes from our home on Bullard Ave, so whether I would drive or walk was a toss-up. I drove. I joined Greg, Thomas, Patrick, and Nathan at the kitchen table when I got there.

Patrick mentioned how much he was looking forward to being together and rafting. "You know, I've done a few floats and low-key rafting. Not like whitewater, though."

"They're providing everything—food, grog, wetsuits, lifejackets, and whatever we'll need on the river," Thomas said.

"Yeah, and we know these guys," Patrick said. "I trust the owner will have everything covered."

"Who's paying for all this?" I asked. I was expecting an overnight adventure with two days of rafting to cost a somewhat substantial sum, and I wanted to be prepared.

"I've got this," Thomas said. "I just had a huge escrow close, and I'm way ahead of the game! You guys can thank me later! But you'll all need sleeping bags and air mattresses—we'll be on the ground. The weather is expected to be nice, but the nights can get cold. At least it's not going to rain!"

"This is too easy," I said. "Looks like we saddle up here Thursday, around noon, and head on up. Everybody okay with that? Anybody need a sleeping bag?" Nobody did.

We would drive in two cars, get there before sundown, and settle in for dinner in front of the campfire. It would take about four hours to drive there, so noon was a good time to start. Additionally, this was a group package, and we didn't know how many others would be joining us. I told the boys, "We don't want to park in the weeds with ass-end Charlie." I laughed at the boys' faces, all looking like I'd lost my mind. I had to explain.

"When your grandfather flew B-17 bombers in WWII, their formations would be huge. The German fighters would avoid attacking the middle of the formation because of each bomber's formidable firepower. They would, instead, pick off the last aircraft in the formation; hence, 'ass-end Charlie' was designated for a straggling American aircraft. In his diary, he mentioned fearing being stuck as ass-end Charlie on missions."

The look of stupefaction on their faces was priceless.

Chapter 2
INCREDIBLE PALETTE OF BRIGHT STARS
Thursday, May 25, 2006

Since Thomas lived in a cul-de-sac, parking was limited. The city required you to park parallel to the curb, ostensibly so that a fire truck can turn around in the cul-de-sac; even though it is small, with only two other houses on it, there still isn't enough curb to park there. So we parked at Nathan's house, three houses down the cross street. The boys were already there, and Nathan's wife, Theresa, had fixed sandwiches for us to eat on the drive. I arrived just before noon.

"I've got dibs on the peanut butter and honey ones!" I said, as she brought them out for us.

"There are plenty of those, some bologna, and some surprises," Theresa said.

"Thanks, honey. Wonderful going-away present!" Nathan climbed into my Yukon, his green eyes crinkling with excitement.

I had thrown two sleeping bags, my air mattress, and some blankets into the back of the car, and after the boys had packed in their gear, we were ready.

Thomas and Michael were already in Thomas's car and ready to go, so Nathan, Greg, and Patrick hopped into my SUV, and we rolled out.

We drove down Highway 99 to the 180 interchange and headed east, not setting any speed records and relaxing as we ate Theresa's sandwiches, which we quickly divided among us. I nibbled on a PB&H, which was substantial and delicious. The weather was perfect and calm, with blue sky and temperatures in the nineties, but traffic was inconsequential.

As we passed through Fresno and approached Academy Boulevard—the only four-way stop on the drive—we saw a small restaurant and a gas station. We considered stopping.

"You guys wanna get something to eat or visit the latrine?" Thomas asked via cellphone.

Nobody wanted to stop, so I replied, "Nope. We're eager to get to King's River Expeditions—no sense in stopping if we don't need to."

From there, the suburban Fresno countryside gave way to vineyards and orange groves. Two months earlier, the orange trees were blossoming, and the whole area was heavy with the pungent fragrance of their blooms, one of my favorite times of the year. Exeter, where I grew up, is surrounded by orange groves, and I've come to appreciate how special the scent is. Now, in May, it lingers a little but only as a memory. However, Belmont Ave is part of the Blossom Trail, which highlights many fruit florets at various times in early spring. Like the orange blossoms, though, they're mostly a memory now. Traffic becomes much more congested in the spring, as families traveling through take advantage of the flowering countryside route.

As we proceeded east, the vineyards and orchards gave way to open rangeland. The rocky ground isn't conducive to agriculture, so livestock, mostly beef, became the scenery. The wandering street finally became Trimmer Springs Road as it skirted the northern edge of Pine Flat Lake. We began to gain elevation slightly, and the scenery became open fields, occasionally interspersed with almond or orange trees.

As a member of the American Legion in Fresno and its motorcycle group, "American Legion Riders," I've taken this road many times. The easy turns and pretty scenery make it a great motorcycle ride. An American Legion chapter met at the lake restaurant off the boat ramp for hot dogs and burgers. We would meet there a few times every summer.

The boat ramp was usually quite busy this time of year, as the docking spots along the ramp were filling up with recreational boats. Fishing and water skiing were very popular when the lake was full, and with full-blown snowmelt happening, that wouldn't take long. The lake was pretty big, but knowing how hard the Kings River rushes into it, I had always been leery of waterskiing there because of the brush—trees, branches, bushes, etc.—that the roaring river carries into it. Skiing would be a real drag for the skier and the boat. Later in the summer, after the river died down, most of that stuff had washed ashore or sunk, so boating wasn't perilous.

"That little diner there is where the American Legion folks hang out when they know we're coming," I said. I pointed to the little shed nestled in the trees. "We can check it out on the way home. It's pretty cool."

We continued along the lake's edge until the road bifurcated, with the left turn leading up to Dinkey Creek and the right continuing around the lake. We took the right turn. The road got narrower and rougher with potholes, finally going over one small creek and another flowing into the lake.

"Thomas, you've driven this before?" I asked. We had kept the phone call open between the two cars.

"Yeah, once by myself and then several times with you and the family when we came up here to float on water mattresses with the Robinsons. It's hard to get lost—there aren't any other roads."

That was the last phone communication we would have with anyone until Saturday afternoon, when we were on our way back home. Once we passed the lake and followed the river, we were actually in Kings Canyon. No radio or cell phone communications were possible because the Canyon's high walls blocked them.

The road was getting very curvy, so we slowed to twenty-five again. I was expecting this and had shared it with the boys when making our plans, so we'd built plenty of time into our schedule to get there.

After about an hour, we came to a small wooden bridge, one-way only, that spanned the river on our right. The river, at this point, was probably thirty feet wide. However, the water crashing beneath it was high, about ten feet below the bridge. I was taken aback because we'd be stranded on the other side if the water got much higher. But I guessed that since the bridge was old, it had weathered this plenty of times.

We crossed over and followed the arrows to the KRE camp. It was a short drive to a flat dirt parking area, where we found easy parking. There were already maybe twenty cars there, so there was plenty of space, and we could stay out of the weeds. That would have been my big concern if I had to sleep on the ground because that's where you'd probably find all kinds of creatures, such as snakes, that live in dense grass. We later discovered that several porta-potties and two large shipping containers, stocked with camping supplies and wetsuits, were located on the edge of the parking lot.

We eased into a parallel parking space next to a big Chevy van and a VW bug, staking out space between our cars for sleeping.

We reconnoitered our location and wandered over to the bonfire amphitheater, which we hadn't seen as we drove in. It was late afternoon, and many people were milling around, visiting. We joined them, finding a few acquaintances along the way. Of course, to my surprise, my boys knew pretty much everybody. They had been instrumental in elevating Central High to recognition in the Tri-River League through their success in volleyball and basketball, making them well-known in the sports community. I've always been amazed by how many people "knew" me because they knew my kids!

The other campers were very friendly, so we immediately felt comfortable. Few children were there, but mostly folks in their twenties and thirties, and a few geezers like me in my late fifties. My little brother, Gordie, his son, and several of the boys' friends we knew were already there. Later, I discovered, judging from the eighteen rafts on the river, that there were more than eighty-four rafters. The staff who cared for us numbered at least thirty. Between the river guides on each raft, the crew that sets up the rafts at drop-off, the cleanup crew, and the organizational cadre that makes it all work seamlessly, this was a very skilled and well-run operation. As an entrepreneur, I was impressed by how well they had put this together.

Around 5:00 p.m., the sun started to set. In the Canyon, the horizon disappears quickly as the sun begins its trek down to the Pacific Ocean, and it gets dark much sooner than we're used to. I found the early sunset unusual but pleasant.

The KRE staff had set up a large table in front of the amphitheater for serving dinner and brought out big roasters with fried chicken, pulled pork, chili beans, green beans with bacon, and a huge salad that any hungry camper would appreciate. What a spread! They even had boxes of red and white wine for anybody who wanted some.

"Hey, you guys hungry?" I asked. My kids were still enjoying their conversations with the other campers. "You know what happens when you're last in line!" They immediately grabbed their plates and got into the buffet queue. Pretty soon, we were all sitting on the amphitheater's logs, enjoying a fine repast. My boys were all big eaters, so they went for seconds, since there was plenty to go around.

Jeb and Julie were the owners of KRE and were highly regarded by their staff. I had been expecting Jeb to be a mountain man type, a codger with a white, grizzled beard. But they were a young couple in their early thirties, athletic, and very pleasant. They were exceptionally well organized and thoughtful, going out of their way to cover all the bases for their guests.

Jeb announced to the assembled diners that they'd fire up the campfire the next night and have dinner a little sooner, as they had some entertainment scheduled for them. Breakfast would be at 7:00 a.m., so we needed to cash in and get a good night's sleep.

When it became apparent that everyone had eaten and we were all done, we sauntered off to our cars and got to work inflating air mattresses. The boys were spread out between our two vehicles, and we were each able to be comfortable.

"Mike, you're gonna wish you had another blanket!" I said. "We have some more in the car, if you want to get one, because we'll probably be covered with frost in the morning!" The taller kids always needed another blanket because their heads stuck out of the sleeping bags, which were never long enough—a common problem my kids were all accustomed to. It was hard for people over six feet tall to find sleeping bags.

It was eight p.m. and already pretty chilly. With darkness descending on the Canyon, we could lie there and look at the amazingly clear sky, studded with an incredible palette of bright stars. Still, even though we weren't exhausted, we fell asleep immediately. Because only a few of us had done any serious rafting before, especially in the Kings during the legendary snowmelt, tomorrow would surely be the beginning of a new and exciting chapter.

As I started to drift off to sleep, it occurred to me that there were times when I wondered if I would survive doing a trip like this with my boys, here in the wilderness, where we were free from machines and technology. However, I had been a businessman, and some of my ventures had appeared hazardous to my life.

I thought back to when I bought a new installation machine for my fledgling insulation business.

Chapter 3
FLASHBACK: MAN AGAINST MACHINE
1975

After having my home in Fullerton insulated in 1975, I moved to Fresno and opened an insulation company. It was clear that home-builders statewide didn't understand the power of proper insulation or the benefits it would provide. After floundering for a year, I finally acquired a truck and began selling and installing insulation myself. I knew that if people could experience the difference in comfort and reduced utility bills, they would not regret it.

When inspecting people's attics as part of providing bids, I found a variety of materials, typically layered to a depth of two inches, including gypsum, vermiculite, rock wool, shredded redwood bark, and old fiberglass, along with rodent trails, among others. The new standard was R-19, which required either nine inches of blown fiberglass or five inches of cellulose—newspaper ground up with boric acid to make it fire-retardant. I preferred cellulose because a roof could burn off without penetrating it, whereas fiberglass would melt.

A company near Sacramento developed an insulation installation machine, which I thought was a promising start, so I purchased one. It had a long, two-and-a-half-inch hose, an electric 220V motor that powered a Roots 150 blower, delivering 150 cubic feet of air per minute, and was superior to any of the others I'd seen. When I came to a home to insulate it, I had to hook up to either their 220V connection in the washroom or their power fuse box. It was an inconvenience, but it worked. The hopper, where the insulation was dumped, could hold two forty-pound bags, which was adequate. Eventually, I had a small electric generator mounted under my truck, which powered the machine.

The Roots blower was sufficient too. It blew the stream of insulation slowly enough that I could install it uniformly, evenly, and to the proper depth. Before long, I had developed a reputation with the PG&E inspectors for doing excellent work.

PG&E, our utility company, launched an energy conservation program for all its customers, offering eight percent financing for insulation. If you were one of their customers, you qualified for financing. I put an ad in the paper and started getting calls for estimates soon after. I would go out in the evening, give estimates, and spend the next day installing what I'd sold. After the job was completed, I'd send the paperwork to PG&E. They'd send their inspector out to check the work. When the check arrived at the homeowner's address a week later, I'd return to retrieve it and see how they appreciated the different comfort level. It was a lot of work, but I was proud of the results. Although our finances were quite tight, I was able to provide a living for my growing family.

One day, I was approached by a door-to-door insulation salesman named Terry Pickard at my small warehouse in Clovis. "I'm looking for a contractor to install the jobs I sell, and they say you have a pretty good reputation. How many jobs can you do in a day?" he asked.

"I can do two on a good day, if my helper isn't sick and the weather is good."

"I sell three a day, and my friend Ted sells two. We're desperate for good installations where PG&E won't 'gig' (fault) the contractor and keep us from receiving the check. You don't have any gigs, and that's amazing. What if you had a machine that one man could operate, and it would blow four attics a day—would you be interested?"

"I've never heard of one that could do that," I said.

"I have a friend who has designed and built one, and you'd be the first to use it. I can have him come and demo it for you tomorrow." Terry was pretty insistent, and I was curious. *He's talking about twenty-five attics a week! I've been doing six a week. This could go somewhere!*

"Okay, I'm not installing any attics tomorrow. If he can do it, I'm game."

Terry called later and confirmed our meeting for 7:00 a.m. the next day.

We met at the warehouse. The machine, made by Viking Manufacturing and called "Mach I," could be built into the back of a fourteen-foot bobtail truck like mine! The bin for the insulation was five feet wide, four feet high, and eight feet long. It had a "live floor," which meant it slowly and incrementally moved whatever was in the bin toward the back of the truck. At the back of the bin was a trough, over which was a chrome-moly shaft with fifteen-inch metal blades, welded every four inches around the shaft. They were called "breaker bars." Below the breakers in the trough was a twelve-inch worm screw traversing the width of the bin to move whatever was in it—insulation—to the "fluffer," which was a box mounted level with the floor at the end of the trough. In the fluffer box was a shaft on which ten-inch blades were mounted. Whatever went into the fluffer would be shredded and dropped into a five-bladed paddle-wheel chamber, which rotated, moving insulation into the stream of air coming from the Roots 300 blower and into the three-inch hose, which went up to the installer in the attic. At the end of the hose was a controller that started or stopped the entire process.

These components were all driven by a single hydraulic pump and operated via a shaft that engaged the truck engine, known as a "power take-off" (PTO). Put the truck transmission in neutral, set the engine RPMs (revolutions per minute) at 1200, engage the PTO, and all the components go into action.

The beauty of hydraulic motors is that they're amazingly powerful and can be set to run at different speeds. The live floor was very slow; the breaker was a little faster; the worm screw was about the same speed as the breakers; the fluffer was very fast; and the paddle was constant and kept in sync with the Roots blower. The Roots delivered three hundred cubic feet of air per minute, twice what I used to.

To demonstrate its capabilities, Terry had them load the hopper with a bale of insulation, several gallon wine bottles, and a bag of beer cans. They explained that the breaker bars would keep turning unless they encountered something they couldn't grind (e.g., a two-by-four, a log, or a concrete block). At this point, the hydraulic pump will enter bypass mode. It stops when the resistance exceeds 1,400 pounds. That prevents it from shearing shafts or bending blades, giving you time to shut down the system and remove the obstruction.

So he turned it on and blew the stuff in the hopper into my large dumpster. It was remarkable. The glass and cans were easily shredded into tiny pieces, mixed into the insulation, and it was all gone within two minutes. Phenomenal! A little noisy but amazing. *Whoa, this is a complete game-changer! I gotta have one!*

The entire concept for this machine was modeled after an agricultural manure spreader. Driving through the fields with a hopper full of manure, the machine would spray the manure in a fan-shaped pattern from the back, delivering it evenly and quickly. To convert it to insulation was tricky but brilliant.

I installed it in my fourteen-foot truck, which was ready to go in a week. My helper, Scott Moore, a former star tackle on FSU's (Fresno State University) football team until he suffered a season-ending knee injury, and I went into action.

Terry Pickard kept his word and delivered many contracts, keeping us busy. I was able to pay for the machine quickly. We could install enough insulation in the truck to cover three houses, and sometimes we'd return to the warehouse to load up for more. It was, indeed, a game-changer for me.

One February morning, we saddled up at 7:00 a.m. to install an attic in Tarpey Village, east of Fresno. It was cold, and my funky old truck engine had a broken choke switch. Scott and I had taken the air cleaner off the carburetor and would choke it ourselves by one of us cutting the air flow with a hand while the other hit the gas. It was easy and something we had to do regularly on cold mornings, but it took two of us, so we weren't doing solo jobs yet.

Scott pulled attic duty this time, so we got him set up with the hose, and I returned to the truck. I put ten forty-pound bags of insulation in the hopper and was ready to add twelve more, which is what the attic would need. With the engine at 1200 RPM, I engaged the PTO. It was now up to Scott. He pushed the button on the controller, and we were off to the races.

I got into the back of the truck and began loading more bags into the hopper. However, for some reason, the insulation was piling up at the right corner of the hopper above the fluffer, so it needed to be slightly evened out to prevent clogging. I used a five-foot-long one-by-four wooden paddle for that, since it happened frequently, and I would redistribute the pile away from the fluffer. Easy. Only this time, it clogged excessively. I climbed into the hopper, up to my knees in insulation—no big deal, since the live floor was moving very slowly—and started pushing the insulation away from the fluffer. But the fluffer caught the end of my paddle and began pulling it away from me. I wrestled with it for a moment, but it pulled hard again, causing me to let go and lose my balance. I regained my balance by leaning my left shoulder against the back wall of the machine, with my right foot propping me up and my left foot lifted above the breakers. Then I grabbed the paddle, but it was immediately and violently jerked out of my hands again.

My left foot dropped, and a breaker bar pierced my calf. It was pulling me down into the worm screw—it even pulled my shoe off and was sending it to the shredder. I reached into the insulation, grabbed the next breaker bar, and pulled up with all my might, in adrenaline mode, to try to stop it. The system went into bypass, which meant I was exerting fourteen hundred pounds of resistance. Suddenly, I knew this was the end because I couldn't hold on for more than five more seconds. If I let go, the system would start up again, and the worm screw would cut off my foot. I would be pulled onto the breakers horizontally, pierced, fed into the worm screw, and delivered into the fluffer. I would quickly become small pieces going up the hose to the attic.

With the hydraulics whining in bypass, the truck engine choked, almost stopped, but gagged, gasped, and suddenly stopped. It made the same unmistakable sound that I've heard a dozen times when I've choked it too much by cupping my hand over the carburetor. It was beyond eerie because I was out of time, and I had almost given up. Stopping the engine was the only way to stop the machine, and it came to a complete halt. For the record, that had never happened before, and it never happened again. I am positive my guardian angel stopped the engine.

With the machine finally off, I pushed down on the breaker bar, bent it sideways, extracted my calf, then rolled over the edge of the bin and dropped out of the back of the truck. I collapsed on the front lawn, wearing a poplin jumpsuit, saturated with sweat, despite the temperature being about sixty degrees. Covered in blood, I wasn't screaming, as the adrenaline overwhelmed me, and I wasn't feeling much pain.

Still in the attic, Scott knew something was wrong, so he ran down to the truck like a flash.

"Thom, what the hell did you do? Are you okay?" Scott lifted me like a rag doll and wrapped a T-shirt around my calf, which was still bleeding profusely.

"I think we need to get him to the hospital right away," Mr. Johnson, the homeowner, said. "Let's get him in my station wagon over there."

Scott picked me up and carried me to the car. They took me to Clovis Community Hospital's emergency room, where the physician and a nurse worked on me for about three hours, cleaning insulation out of the six-inch-long wound in my left calf and stitching it. When they were done, my wife, Kelly, picked me up. They issued me a pair of crutches to help me get around and sent me home.

Kelly put me in bed and, conferring with Scott, took care of everything else. My mother-in-law, June Chamberlin, dropped in the next day to visit. She brought me a book: Corrie ten Boom's "Prayers & Promises for Every Day," which was heartwarming.

I've always appreciated Corrie's story and the walk with God that she shares in her profound writings. This one, though—a daily devotional—was different. The accident happened on February 14. The verse for the next day, February 15, was: "I have saved your life and kept your feet from slipping … so that you may walk before the Lord in the land of the living." (Psalm 56:13) I was utterly overcome with awe. God was talking to me through Corrie. The bit about feet slipping was just over the top. My right foot hadn't slipped, but if it had, it would have been game over!

Interesting footnote: most of the Psalms are about things God *will do* (future tense) and what His people *ask Him to do*. But this is about what He *did* (in the past perfect tense). This shook me to the core and still makes me break down in tears.

My brother-in-law, Chuck Aston, took a month off from his job as a probation officer and assumed my position with Scott. He kept the business alive until I recovered, and I am eternally grateful.

To prevent this from ever happening again, we installed a kill switch at the hopper.

The bill from Clovis Community was something I had been dreading because I expected it to be more than $ 2,500. In college, I worked in the business office of Kaweah Delta District Hospital in Visalia, so I knew what kind of bill to expect! We didn't have workers' compensation, and insurance didn't cover me. We were concerned about every dollar we spent. But the bill was $185.00. There was no explanation for it. Just a very low charge. Another gift from God!

Chapter 4
WE WILL GET WET!
Friday, May 26, 2006

What a night. I had fallen asleep, grateful to enjoy the wilderness with my children again, realizing we can't take anything for granted. But my air mattress, which I was sure had no leaks, deflated completely sometime before 4:00 a.m. I thought I had moved all the pesky rocks before I lay out the sleeping bag, but some remained under my shoulders, which were troublesome. Regardless, I got a good seven hours of sleep, which is unusual for me. Still, I was awake as the sun peeked over the Canyon wall. The sunrise in Kings Canyon reminded me of Yosemite, where I'd stayed for three weeks in the 1970s doing an insulation contracting job. It starts to get light very slowly, and then—bang—the sun is right there in your face! It's a unique experience.

It was probably forty-five degrees and quite nippy, with a slight layer of frost accumulated on the blankets covering our sleeping bags. Looking around, I saw the other campers coming to life all at once. My sons were already up and out of sight.

The sturdy metal "gathering" bell mounted on a dark wood post near the parking area sounded at about 6:30 a.m., so I gave myself an insulin shot and strolled over to the amphitheater, where the rafting company set up the breakfast buffet for us. The boys were already in line, and the line was moving quickly.

"You guys must have been working on this for the last couple of hours," I told Julie, KRE co-owner and chef extraordinaire. "This is quite a feast, and I appreciate your choices, like butter and maple syrup!" We filled our plates with scrambled eggs, tons of bacon, and sourdough flapjacks with real butter and maple syrup—just like my wife makes! At my house, Kelly and I presented our family with only foods that met our standards—avoiding preservatives and additives, artificial flavors, and opting for real food. Flapjacks were typically sourdough, from a recipe and starter my mother had given me many years ago, and real maple syrup—not the junk with corn sugar and other stuff. Pure maple syrup, we taught our kids, is good for you. I felt like we were going home with this breakfast—my kind of stuff! We're used to being in a league of our own, with different standards, from the moment we started having kids. She would appreciate what Julie did for her boys.

"We have a system that works well," Julie said. "We fix the complicated stuff in Fresno and then warm it up here. It's easy."

"Wow, it looks fresh like you just cooked it, and it's got to taste great!" I said.

She agreed, adding, "It's amazing how good food tastes when it's cold out and you're hungry!" And we were both cold and hungry.

Jeb, Julie's spouse and the rafting company's co-owner, addressed all the campers still in the amphitheater, which was most of them.

"Hey folks, please drop by the CONEX—that shipping container where the wetsuits and life jackets are stored," Jeb said. He pointed to the structure to the east of where we were eating. "You each need a top, pants, and booties for the wetsuit. Life jackets will be in the rafts, which we've already taken to the drop-off point where rafting will start. We'll briefly discuss rafting safety when you're all on the bus. We need to be sure we're all on the same page regarding rafting etiquette and some things to watch out for." We all nodded to confirm that we would.

"Listen, the water temperature is in the low forties since it's from fresh snowmelt, and without a wetsuit, it could be extremely uncomfortable if you had to swim. So get comfortable in the wetsuit!"

Once we were outfitted, we returned to the car to leave our jackets and other belongings. I was surprised at how warm my whole body felt after putting on the wetsuit—it felt just perfect, despite the cold morning air. However, the sun was quickly warming the area, so we were eager to start the party!

By 9:30 a.m., we were all walking around like penguins in our wetsuits, but the boys were getting antsy, waiting for the bus Jeb had said would take us up the river to the drop-off point. In no time, the old school bus rumbled up the dusty road, turned around, stopped, and waited for us as if on cue. It was one of those old-style school buses with the engine in the front and a hood. It had a three-speed transmission that required double-clutching, which isn't a big deal once you get used to it. You push the clutch in to take it out of gear, then push it back in when ready to move into the next gear.

"Being all decked out in wetsuits, I bet we could go surfing on the river if we had our surfboards!" Patrick said.

"It wouldn't work," Nathan said to Patrick. "But I saw Jeb with a one-person kayak in his pickup. Bet he'll be running the rapids behind us today."

We filed into the bus, took seats, and waited. The whole bus filled up with our group, and when we were all on board, Jeb stuck his head in for a brief word.

"It's quite a curvy drive to get up where we need to go, so if anyone gets carsick, trade with someone in the front seats. The secret to not getting too sick is watching the road, not the trees. Getting up there takes about an hour, so be aware and take your time. If you have any problems, tell Jack, our bus driver here, and he'll try to help out." He ducked out and got in his pickup to follow us.

Lordy, an hour? With a manual transmission, this old school bus will get a workout.

"Hey, Jack," someone in the back called out. "Have you been doing this long?"

"I've worked for KRE for three years now, and driving this bus is one of the many things I get to do," he said. "Other than learning to double-clutch it and not turn too sharply in the corners, it's been fun. I never see anyone coming down when we're going up, so this one-lane road hasn't been too challenging." He was driving like he'd been doing it forever, so I was sure the other passengers were just as confident as I was.

We started down the dusty road toward the bridge, then crossed over to the northern side of the river, where there was a narrow asphalt road between the river and the granite mountain on our left. Jack put the bus in second and bumped along, taking the corners carefully and slowly. The slight elevation change wasn't noticeable. The potholes on the road made it easy to stay alert and focused so that we wouldn't get carsick.

We'd been on the road for about ten minutes when a young lady sitting behind me said, "Jack, I'm starting to get sick."

Jack slowed down a little. We had been moving at about twenty miles per hour—about as fast as one should drive on curves like this—and asked Jeff, sitting behind him in the front row, if he would mind changing seats with her. Jeff didn't flinch. He got up, beckoned to her, and they switched places.

"I don't get carsick," Jeff said, smiling at her. She didn't have a barf bag, so we were glad she had moved. She recovered her composure quickly and didn't seem to have a problem for the rest of the drive.

The curvy road and occasional switchbacks were arduous for all passengers, especially since we'd only finished our substantial breakfast less than two hours before. But we were getting where we needed to go, so we silently put up with it and rolled with the turns.

We passed stands of birch, weeping willows, cedars, and lodgepole pines. We also noticed a lot of buckbrush and manzanita closer to the river. Once in a while, the river was way out of sight, as we wound slowly up through the rocky landscape. The trees and brush looked nondescript, and elevation was the only change. Most of the time, we were higher than the river and could see it below us along the sheer wall that bordered it. But finally, we came to a tight clearing at the river's edge where there was a small bay. About twenty, six-person rafts were in the bay, all tightly moored on a rope stretching across the thirty-foot cove and waiting for passengers.

When we climbed off the bus, Jeb read off a list of who would be in each raft, and I was assigned to one with all five of my sons.

"How come you guys are dressed like you expected to get wet?" I asked. They all had ski goggles, beanies, and hats for head protection—stuff I hadn't even thought to bring.

"Come on, Dad, if we don't get wet, it won't be a real whitewater experience!" Thomas said. "We *will* get wet, and it *will* be fun!"

"Okay, I'm supposed to be a Boy Scout here?" I exclaimed. I held my right hand in the Scout's pledge position. "'Be Prepared' is our motto, and you guys are making me feel a bit old and unprepared!"

"Well, you are old!" Patrick said. He laughed, but then felt a little bad. "But not *too* old!"

"Agreed. At least I have hair, so my head won't freeze!" I said. I looked over at Thomas, who was bald and wearing a jungle hat. My wife's uncle was bald, and that's where Thomas inherited the baldness gene. He was the only one of my kids to get it.

Our guide, Jeff, the one who switched places with the sick woman in the bus, held our raft at the water's edge, and as we scrambled into it, we each took a life jacket from a pile next to the bus. We took up positions arbitrarily because we had no idea what to expect. It turns out we did well—the vigorous paddling in the front was essential, and Thomas and Patrick, who sat there, were the best for that position. The middle and back rows were instrumental with side paddling to reverse or turn, and Greg and Michael made sense in the middle with Nate and me in the back row. Jeff was behind us.

Thomas and Greg pointed out another reason the setup was good.

"Dad's shoulder has a slight injury, and so we expect he won't be a great deal of help," he said. "That's fine because we're all big guys who can do what needs to be done. Of course, we wanted to be challenged. So, Jeff, take us into the most aggressive part of the water and watch us get through it. It'll be a great experience."

"I have a bad shoulder too," Greg said. "I dislocated my right shoulder. So, with me on one side of the boat and Dad on the other, with his bad shoulder, it should work. The cool thing is that our bad shoulders are on the opposite sides, which balances us out."

Jeff had us practice in the little bay where all the rafts were, paddling on command and getting a feel for what happens when one side reverses and the other paddles forward. We would go in a quick circle.

This is going to be fun! It's not that hard. We'll have a blast!

Since we were catching on quickly, Jeff gave the green light, and we were released into the current about three minutes behind the first raft. We all began paddling as instructed. Still in the back and standing, Jeff used his oar like a rudder, directing the nose where he wanted us to go.

He shouted out commands. "Left hard," "right reverse," or "left hold." I was on the left side and listened for his "left" commands. Once we were in the current and headed downriver, the game was on! We were maneuvering around rocks, choosing a trajectory that would lead through tight spaces, and it was exhilarating! The boys were strong, and we powered through some challenging terrain, avoiding numerous crashes with foliage and protruding rocks. At this point, I considered the rapids Class 2—fun but not treacherous. It wasn't deafening and only mildly challenging, which was fine because we had some learning to do before being skilled enough for Class 3.

But I had never been on the river during snowmelt.

Chapter 5
WE DID IT!
Friday, May 26, 2006, 11:15 a.m.

After about half an hour, we reached a section of the river they call "Bonzai Canyon," which is Class 3. It is a point where the river narrows due to rocks on the sides and below, and the water speeds up. I remembered something I learned in college. The Venturi effect, taught in physics, states that when a volume of fluid, such as water, is forced through a constricted area, the speed increases and the pressure decreases, much like turning on a hose nozzle. I hadn't experienced this principle in real life, but it was now right before my eyes!

The faster water, of course, is whitewater! It was cranking, surging, almost growling, and daring us to enter! Our eyes widened as we went straight into it, and our collective stomach muscles tightened. Bonzai Canyon was about a hundred yards long. I could see it all and anticipate what would happen next. There was a drop in elevation, which made us go even faster. *Whoa, we're gonna get wet!*

We went over a few rocks ahead of us and tracked left to right to avoid boulders, which was challenging.

"Hard left! Harder! Right, stop, stop, STOP! Now go forward!" We could barely hear Jeff's voice over the din of the rushing water.

The guys in front were doing all kinds of gymnastics to help steer us away from rocks, and that was great, but our tillerman, Jeff, was hard at work trying to determine our direction. There was a large rock in the middle of the channel that, as we approached, we could see would be a close call. If we hit it wrong, we might capsize.

It was mostly submerged, flat on top, with a smooth water jet flowing over it. Someone called it a "rooster tail." Jeff pointed us right at it, and we were slightly airborne as we went over the rock. It happened so fast that we didn't have time to be worried about "what if," but we made it! We landed flat with a splat in the middle of a large section of whitewater. *That was scary. I hope there aren't more of those further downstream. We could easily have tipped over. So, this is what it's all about!* We got severely splashed and took on some water, but we were exuberant!

The feeling of moving back and forth on the river was similar to skiing. Here we were, looking downstream at the white, turbulent water, with a clear picture of where we had to go. We had to stay upright and balanced, keeping our heads as we navigated the rocks and rougher rapids, much like on a snow-covered mountainside ski slope with moguls and obstacles. Scary, but it was very exciting!

Jeb was right; these wetsuits were a godsend on this trip.

Eventually, as we cleared Bonzai, the river got wider and shallower. It slowed down quite a bit—the Venturi effect again—allowing us to relax a little. Then, I realized how tense I had been for the last twenty minutes, so I could finally take a deep breath and relax my shoulders! We discovered that the river was deeper on the left bank, where the faster flow had cut a channel, so Jeff guided us to move slowly toward it to re-enter the faster current.

"Right, paddle forward," Jeff yelled. "Front, paddle left! Left, reverse!" While we didn't have much experience, we knew what he wanted.

Soon, we were back in some rapids, but nothing quite like Bonzai. Negotiating rocks and staying in the river's center, finding the channel with the fastest flow, was easy, fun, and constant—plenty of mellow rapids without the trauma of Bonzai and never a dull moment.

Finally, we came to a clearing. Except in this spot, the river's edge was lined with brush—bushes my father called "buckbrush." Thick and almost impenetrable when you're on foot, two to four feet high, and with sharp branches—this was the kind of stuff Br'er Rabbit would jump into to get away from Br'er Fox in the storybooks by Uncle Remus. Looking at them now, I recalled the "brambles" in those childhood stories.

During the summer, when the river's depth recedes, there are fishermen's trails along the south side through the buckbrush, which grows uphill toward the walls of the Canyon. The bank is open and without foliage. But when the water rises, the bank disappears, and the river's edge becomes solid buckbrush. Finding a place to pull over and rest, or have lunch, requires knowing the "lay of the land." Our guide was indispensable since he had been doing this for several years.

"Jeff, I'm sure glad you found this spot to take a break because I never would have seen it! We've been so focused on rocks and where the river takes us that we would have gone right by this spot!" Nathan said. "Thomas and Patrick have been working their butts off, and Dad and I have been paddling constantly to try to keep in the direction they're moving us, so this has been a real exercise!"

"Aw, come on, Nate, I saw your eyes in Bonzai—you were freaking out, paddling like a big dog!" said Patrick. "Thank goodness you guys with the paddles were on it because we could have gone sideways twice and done a spectacular upside-down landing! This river is a tricky rascal, sneaking stuff up on you, and damned if we weren't up for it."

"Yeah, I was a little traumatized a couple of times in Bonzai, but I bet we all were!" Nathan said. "Even with a wetsuit, I'm not sure how much fun swimming in today's river would be! I prefer to be in the raft!"

"I think you guys were an amazing team," I said. "This is fun, seeing you working like a well-oiled machine and facing new challenges every other minute. I appreciate the opportunity to see you guys in action! Sure, it was great watching you in volleyball and basketball, but those are sports you have to practice with others—you know, team sports. This experience is completely different. You have to face unexpected challenges head-on and utilize all your skills to overcome them. For me, it's a joy watching you! But I must admit, there isn't much time to be an observer when I'm manning an oar like this."

Thomas grinned. "Dad, we're glad you came. You have to realize that our synergy and skills were inherited from you, so this is a perfect family outing."

We had been sloshing in the water we took on in Bonzai, so when we pulled over for the quick lunch break, we turned the boat over to drain it. Anyone who needed to "drain the lizard" found a tree. There weren't any logs or big rocks to sit on, so we all piled into the raft again to have a sandwich and some of the little bags of Fritos or potato chips that Julie had sent. The sandwiches were all bologna and tasty. The little bottles of water were a nice touch. Interesting how you can get thirsty amid all this cold water! But we were. Drinking river water could have been okay, but we'd been taught in Scouts to avoid drinking from streams because of the parasites possibly introduced into the stream by poop from deer, bears, and other wildlife. So the bottled water was preferable.

Fortunately, the wetsuits protected us from the sun, so sunburn wasn't a concern. And the water in the raft wasn't a big deal because we were all nestled in wetsuits, basically impervious to water. Still, it was the principle of the thing! Moving around was just easier without sitting in five inches of water. After a fifteen-minute respite, we bagged the wrappers and plastic from our lunch, assumed our positions, and continued down the river.

A few more exciting rapids and delicate maneuvering around rocks, and we finally came to our campsite at about 3:30 p.m. We pulled over and docked the raft by tying it to a rope between two trees, leaving room for the other rafts. We were tired but not exhausted, and we were glad to be back.

The rafts down the river were staggered at the start by about four minutes each, and there were eighteen rafts, so that the whole trip would take more than an hour to get all the rafts moving, from first to last. We were the second, so we could watch the others all come in. As they arrived, before we left to change out of our wetsuits, we could tell they had all had a fantastic time with Bonzai, and nobody had flipped! It was a joy to experience the same high level of excitement that we all now appreciated after just a short time in the river. This sense of "we did it!" was pervasive, like we had graduated into a class of experienced rafters.

Just then, one of the rafts pulled in. "So, did you guys get soaked?" Greg asked.

"Oh, hell yes, and it was glorious, and we're stoked!" said one of the new arrivals. "But we had a great time, and I can't wait for tomorrow! We almost flipped a couple of times, but our guide's guidance and teamwork pulled us out of the fire. What a great ride! How'd you guys do?"

"We took on a lot of water but weren't in danger of flipping. It was close a couple of times, but we're getting the hang of it," Greg said.

We hustled through the amphitheater and to the parking lot, where we changed out of our wetsuits and back into street clothes, then put them on our car seats so they would dry in the sun. It was pretty warm—about ninety degrees—so it was T-shirt weather again.

The cadre at KRE was like family, and we could feel the togetherness and affection they all shared. What a unique experience we had, making the trip even more unforgettable because we fit together so comfortably. You'd think that with these many strangers together in semi-harsh conditions, some conflicts might have popped up here and there, but that didn't happen. It was terrific; all the smiles, affection, and sharing—just plain happiness spread among us.

At 6:30 p.m., the sun was setting, the temperature was dropping fast, and we were hungry! The crew brought out the dinner. Julie had served roasted chicken, sliced beef with gravy, fresh green beans with almond slivers (not the type typically served at fundraisers, but delicious green beans nonetheless), chili beans, and slices of toasted garlic bread. It was a satisfying dinner for hungry rafters. We were smiling the whole time.

We lined up and dished out what we wanted, chatting and comparing notes about the river, while the staff brought out more wood for the campfire and got it going. We sat on the halved logs in the amphitheater, enjoying a fine dinner while the fire intensified. The rafters were very comfortable in a campfire setting like this, with paper plates and no tables and chairs. The temperature had already dropped from the eighties to the low seventies, so that premium Gallo boxed wine helped to provide a little warmth!

The staff had a few skits planned for the "stage." Try to picture logs, placed in a five-level semicircle, accommodating maybe eighty or more people. The area in the center was like a small stage in front of the bonfire, which was raised about four feet high. Once we'd finished eating and sipping wine, the entertainment crew came on. We sang a few songs, such as "This Land is Your Land" and some easy camp tunes. Then we watched a humorous skit about the frontier, which I don't remember. Last came a storyteller.

In my campfire days with the Boy Scouts, with the temperature dropping and everyone full of food and grog, this would have been a grand opportunity to scare the bejeebers out of all the campers. It reminded me of when my dad told Yeti stories that were so real and scary that the guys around the campfire were afraid to return to their tents! But this was more of a historical story about the Kings River and the Yokut Indians. I've always felt that the Yokuts were connected to the land in ways we don't understand. I have long been eager to learn more about their experience.

But this story was about domination and death, and my feelings were somewhat subdued. Early settlers coming into the valley considered the Yokuts to be aborigines and treated them as if they were barely human, often wiping out whole tribes to take their land. Since they couldn't fight back against the guns the settlers used, it was wholesale slaughter. The pride and cultural history of the Yokuts were being erased, and I didn't see how this could be considered anything but detrimental to their heritage. This part of our history isn't often told, and tonight the storyteller skipped much of the gore. I was okay with that, because I'd read Frank Latta's book, *Handbook of Yokuts Indians*, and I knew this wasn't a happy story with a happy ending. I couldn't see the value of the presentation, except for the fact that it discussed the Canyon's prior inhabitants. Now they were all gone, living like ghosts in the shadows and in the memories of those who knew about them.

I was inducted into the Boy Scouts Order of the Arrow, an elite group that offered traditional Native American experiences, including cooking and first aid, among other activities. We developed a great deal of respect and became familiar with many of the Yokuts' customs and practices. I quickly came to respect them. They had learned to survive the harsh summers of the San Joaquin Valley, and there are many lessons we could understand and appreciate from their experience.

For example, it's hard not to admire their skill in basketweaving, developed over many generations. Using shredded tules and grasses, they would weave large, beautiful baskets so tight they were waterproof. By placing hot rocks in a basket of water, they could easily cook dinner for the whole family using acorn flour and perhaps a rabbit or two. Another interesting custom I found helpful was to avoid the oaks, which dotted the arid landscape, beckoning travelers to find respite in the shade. Livestock would gravitate to that shade. But invariably the ticks, fleas, and flies that accompanied the livestock were also enjoying that shade—enter at your peril!

In a flash, it was 8:00 p.m. and time for bed. We were all tired and scrambled off to our sleeping bags. In my case, I had to blow up the air mattress again and hope it didn't deflate before I fell asleep.

"Greg, are you fitting in the sleeping bag?" I asked.

"Yeah, I have to curl up a little, but it works. I don't have any rocks under me, so it's very comfortable. I'll throw a towel over my head this time, because if I get a cramp, I'll need to stretch out, and I'll be sticking out too far."

"You worried about cramps?"

"Yeah, after being folded up in the raft for so long. Michael and I both have circulation issues to consider. When we were both involved in volleyball and basketball, we were fine every day, but after a brief layoff, cramps sometimes came as a surprise. I suppose it happens to anyone who's a serious athlete."

"Good grief, I didn't know that." I shook my head.

"My legs are just fine now," Michael said. "But I hear you, Greg, it's a stinker when a cramp sneaks up on you. But I'm going to sleep like a rock tonight."

Nathan was deep in thought. "Going through Bonzai today was a trip that worried me a little. If the raft had flipped and we had to swim for it, that would have been some nasty water. We're all swimmers, and normally, swimming in a river is no big deal, but this is different."

"Aw, Nate, this experience is so magical that it'll be a slam-dunk. I'm enjoying whatever the river throws at us!" Patrick was always our optimist.

Day one of whitewater rafting on the King's River, May 26, 2006! From front to back, left to right: Michael and Thomas, Greg and me, Nathan and Patrick, with Jeff, our guide and tiller, in the very back.

Chapter 6
THE BEAST OF BONZAI
Saturday, May 27, 2006, 7:00 a.m.

It was about five degrees cooler on Friday night than the night before. Saturday morning, we woke up to find our sleeping bags frostier than expected, covered with a fine layer of ice crystals, but we looked up to another beautiful, clear sky. Jeb had told us before we went to bed that colder nights meant less snowmelt, so we should expect the river to be a little different from the day before. I couldn't imagine how that would matter much, since the river was turbulent no matter what, but we would soon see.

When the food bell rang, we began assembling in the amphitheater, where three tables had been set up for a fantastic array of breakfast. We chatted with the other campers while we cruised through the food line. Scrambled eggs, bacon, sausage, toast, oatmeal, little single servings of Kellogg's cereals—all you can eat—and strong camp coffee were provided. Good stuff.

"You guys see anything fun yesterday?" asked Nick French. He spoke to the brothers and me as we casually sat on the half-logs in the amphitheater and enjoyed our breakfast. I don't usually eat breakfast at home, but that's probably because my job is pretty sedentary, and I didn't work up much of an appetite like I did when I was younger. Still, there was nothing like camp breakfasts, and I was thoroughly bent on enjoying this one.

Despite being a great athlete and a stellar basketball player, Nick has never been haughty or cocky. His disposition is respectful and friendly, and he's easy to talk to, which you might not expect from a six-foot-eight superstar. Quickly, you discover that he is intelligent and thoughtful.

"Nick, this whole experience is fun, and we love it!" I said. "It's good to be on the same team with you, for a change. You used to kill us when Central played against you at Clovis West."

"You know, when you're playing inside under the rim, you have to take on a completely different mindset," Nick said. "You must want to dominate and not let anything stand in your way. When I figured that out, I got pretty good. Still, I remember times when Nathan would smoke me, and I'd see red." Nathan and Patrick had played against Nick, and they rolled their eyes at each other upon hearing that.

Nathan chortled. "Yeah, but that didn't happen very often. You ate everyone's lunch as a junior and a senior. We tried everything, but you were so damn fierce!" The respect great athletes have for one another led Nick to grow close to us as part of our athletic family, and he has remained part of it through the years.

"But you know, the scenery on this river is amazing," Nick said. "The trees at the edges, the willows bending in the wind, the leaves of the quaking aspen flashing in the sunlight while being shaken in the breeze, the granite all over the place, looking up at the huge Canyon walls—it's just cool. It's stuff you probably wouldn't normally appreciate, except when you're on an exciting rafting experience like this. Your senses are a level sharper."

"I agree," Patrick said. "I noticed it too. The colors seem brighter, the spray in your face makes you feel more intense, and the whole experience is like you're on steroids. I didn't think it would be this much fun."

"Are you pussies going to sit around and bloviate on esoteric stuff, or are we going to get on with this rafting?" Thomas asked. "Get your wetsuits on, and let's be ready when the school bus arrives!" With his military experience and being the oldest of seven children, he was accustomed to taking charge and directing others.

"Well, alrighty then!" Greg said, trying to sound like comedic actor Jim Carrey.

Nick approached Thomas. "Thomas, is there any way I could switch and ride with your brothers? You know they're all my buddies. And you could take my spot."

Thomas nodded. "Yeah, not a problem. I mean, it's not a big deal to me."

Nick was probably about twenty to thirty pounds heavier than Thomas, but they switched. Nick was now in boat two with us, and Thomas switched to boat thirteen.

I was just along for the ride, and my kids orchestrated the whole adventure for me. I was okay with that, though sometimes, I expressed a cantankerous attitude to throw a wrench into the program or get them to slow down and think things through a little more. I don't condone moving without planning—Boy Scout training and Army experience were part of my MO (method of operation). But this adventure felt like a Scout hike, with the senior patrol leader directing us.

We all moved to our cars and changed into wetsuits. It was a little colder, but it was getting slightly warmer now with the sun out. Wetsuits would be welcome. The air temperature was probably around fifty degrees, although we had no way of knowing. And we didn't care.

The KRE crew rang the bell when the bus arrived to take us to the designated drop-off point at about 9 a.m. We gathered quickly and filed into it with anticipation. The bus's old manual transmission seemed to be tortured, working itself into a grave with grinding, whining, and all kinds of noises, but it kept going! Jack's double-clutching did the trick, and within an hour, we were at the drop-off, just like yesterday.

With Nick switching to my raft, along with Michael, Greg, Nathan, and me, and our new guide, Kevin Davis, a giant man, our raft now weighed significantly more than it had the day before. Kevin could have been a Paul Bunyan lumberjack; my three boys weighed over two hundred and forty pounds each. We'd have a full load. I closed it out at about two fifteen. But we fit well in the raft.

Nathan noticed the extra poundage and verbalized it. "Yesterday, Nick, six feet eight and two hundred and seventy pounds, was not in our boat. Our guide was five feet ten inches tall and weighed one hundred and seventy-five pounds. Today, our guide, Kevin, is huge—a big difference. Our boat has at least one hundred pounds more weight today."

And when we all got in that raft, there was a hint of water at the bottom from our heavier crew weighing it down. I think most of us thought that only meant we might not sail through the water as fast as the day before.

Once we had completed the preparatory skill maneuvers with the paddles—such as the left-side paddle forward and the right-side paddle backward, which made the raft turn quickly in a circle—Kevin was confident that we were on the same page. At around 10:15 a.m., he gave the green light to merge into the river. We were ready and excited!

We paused momentarily and took deep breaths as we looked down the river. It was like being at the top of a steep ski slope, ready to let it rip—only we were in water! Innocuous, exhilarating, but foreboding, we knew extremely frigid and fast-moving water could be dangerous. But we expected to have some serious fun that day.

We soon noticed what Jeb, the owner of KRE, meant when he said the water would be a little lower. Rocks we hadn't seen yesterday were suddenly threatening our passage, requiring more maneuvering than before. It was fun, but more challenging, necessitating paddling we hadn't done during the first day of rafting.

"Left hard paddle, harder, harder—right back, now forward hard!" Kevin exhorted us and steered us through the rocks. This is what whitewater rafting was all about, and we were digging it. Working as a team and navigating treacherous rapids while only getting a slight splash was thrilling and surprising. I expected we would get drenched, but we stayed above it and felt triumphant.

As we approached Bonzai, we were amped up. Expecting it to be the day's big adventure, we could now see that the big rock we had seen yesterday, in the middle, was now not entirely covered by water. But it had a "rooster tail" over the middle of it, right where we were headed, which indicated turbulence in the flow. That meant trouble we didn't have to contend with yesterday. We had no time to think about it; we could only steer to the side and try to avoid it. Kevin tried like crazy to control us, but there was no way to circumvent it. The rushing current carried us straight at it, and as we started over it, the back of our raft sank and the front went up. This was mainly because we had a lot of weight in the rear, even though we thought it was well distributed. Still, it was much heavier than the day before.

We started tipping. Kevin shouted, "The raft is going to flip!"

We're all going to be thrown off this raft!

"I can't believe this," Nathan shouted.

Kevin was right. We hit the rock hard, and it flipped the raft, front to back. We were all ejected. Nathan and I flew to the right into mid-stream, and everyone else went to the left, toward the bank, where the strongest part of the current was.

When I first hit the water, I shouted, "Bring it on!" because I figured the wetsuit and lifejacket would keep me safe. How cool to be buoyed in the river and experience the power of the water with relative impunity.

Within ten seconds, I was swallowing my words. The whitewater waves were crashing over me and overwhelming me. I had figured I could face the waves and they'd go around me. Baloney. Water is a formidable force and deserves tremendous respect, especially since we're not water creatures like trout. Water weighs eight pounds per gallon, and hundreds—maybe thousands—of gallons were coming at me all at once.

Somehow, I had never considered the weight and force of the rushing river, especially when it's icy cold, and I would have to fight like crazy to keep my head above the onslaught of waves constantly breaking over me. It was suddenly obvious I was overwhelmed, outmanned, and inadequate, and I didn't have a plan to save myself. I couldn't swim in the river because it was towering over me, pounding, and submerging me. It took all my strength to keep my head above the whitewater, and I was growing increasingly cold, making it difficult to catch my breath.

I realized that Nathan and I were caught in a keeper, much larger and more powerful than the one that had almost drowned my friend in the ditch. Seeing Nathan struggling, I was concerned but couldn't reach him. I kept getting pulled down, and when I resurfaced, I lost my bearings.

I heard Nathan screaming, "Dad! Dad, I see you! Can you see me?"

I looked in the direction of his voice and saw Nathan bobbing in the whitewater to my left. But before I could shout an encouraging word, I was pulled back under. I feared we were both doomed if he was experiencing what I was.

At last, I came up for air, and we were looking straight at each other. I saw the same panic in his eyes that I felt. A wave hit us both and pulled me back under the water. Nathan came down after me, but he couldn't reach me and was pushed back to the top. I was running out of air, and it took all of my strength not to panic.

Nathan's Perspective

My dad and I were caught in a powerful keeper. Neither of us was in control. We caught sight of each other and then were separated by the force of the water. We looked at each other, wondering if we would make it.

I've heard enough about keepers to know that fighting their force is a losing battle. So the general advice is to let go. Quit fighting. However, being sucked into the abyss is not something that our human instincts will allow. So, I fought it at first. Fortunately for me, once I remembered and let go, the keeper ejected me, and my life jacket returned me to the top.

I didn't know where my dad was. But I'm thinking, if I don't dash for the shore right now, I'm going down the cycle for another hour, and I'll die. So, I swam as hard as I could to the river's edge, something like one hundred and fifty yards. I lay there, holding onto a rock, waiting.

I told myself that my dad would not let himself drown. It wasn't in his nature to give up. I wondered how long it would be before he got shot out of the keeper like I did. I kept looking for him to appear. But he didn't, and I feared the worst.

Thom's Perspective

I got my head above water by constantly kicking. I was swept to the right bank, where a large rock was blocking the flow. *Maybe I can grab onto a ledge on the rock and pull myself out of the rapids.* But as I reached for the ledge, I was immediately pulled down. Straight down, maybe ten feet. The suddenness surprised me, as if someone were pulling on my legs and feet.

I held my breath and fought to get to the top. I was impressed by how quickly the freezing water sapped my energy, even though I had expected the wetsuit to better maintain my body temperature. Still, wetsuits were meant only as a stopgap measure that lasted maybe ten minutes. After that, I knew that once my body was at water temperature, the game was over.

A sense of doom pressed against me as I fought demons that were threatening to take my life. I suddenly had terrible feelings about what the river could do, despite my pride in my skill with watersports. Yet, I refused to give up the fight. *Lord, I'm not sure I can do this. Please give me strength. I don't think I'll be able to make it.*

Abruptly, I was pushed to the surface and popped out for just a second. I was able to get a full breath before I was yanked down again.

The downward current was so strong that it pulled my booties off before it shoved me up again. This up-and-down cycle occurred perhaps four times, but I was able to take a partial breath with each. However, I was running out of time.

The cold water made it extremely difficult to breathe, further exacerbated by exhaustion. Since I was in survival mode, I wasn't thinking about any action I could take that could end this; instead, my body was responding to stimuli without any conscious thought from me—tit for tat, period. Panic set in, so it was a matter of whether I could react to the next challenge.

I anticipated popping out in the next cycle and getting a full breath of air. As I was pushed up again, I began letting my air out to have room for a lungful of oxygen. I was looking up and was about a foot from the surface, surging with all my might—even today I can still see that surface just above me—with no air in my lungs and expecting to burst out and get a deep breath. But the keeper suddenly pulled me down. With nothing in my lungs, I instinctively inhaled, taking in water.

I was instantly unconscious.

Chapter 7
GRAB THE ROPE
Saturday, May 27, 2006, 10:50 a.m.

Gordie's Perspective

My son, Jeremy, and I were at the front of our raft, which was the first one in the water that day. Our guide, Stacey Serra, turned around and saw that the raft behind us had capsized, and men had gone overboard. Fortunately for us, the river widened at that spot, creating a small area where the water becomes much shallower and the current slows. We pulled out of the faster-moving current and into a little bay against the willows. It wasn't a large area, just big enough for a few rafts. Three men in our raft held onto the buckbrush at the edge to maintain our position while we watched for those in the water.

We waited there. The faster channel of the river, flowing as fast as Bonzai, courses to the south bank, to our left, where it has gouged a deeper, narrower track.

Stacey said that those in the capsized raft would float down to us, probably very near our raft. We prepared to fish them out of the current. My nephew, Thom's son Michael, was the first one floating down the river to reach ours. That's when I realized that it was my brother's raft that turned over.

I helped pull Michael aboard, who was visibly shaking. “Michael, are you okay?” I asked.

“Everybody's flailing around in the water, Uncle Gordie. I was hit by several waves and thought I wasn't going to make it!”

I put my hand on his shoulder to calm him, my concern for Thom growing.

“It's incredible how quickly the cold water saps your strength,” Michael said. “Plus, with the beating my body was taking from the forces of the waves, I thought I was toast. After being hit by the last couple of waves, I didn't even have the strength to get my arms up and try to make it to the side where I could pull myself up and out of the water. I just let those waves hit me in the face as I was pushed downstream. I was so relieved to see your raft pulled over to the side. My legs are frozen from being in this icy cold water for so long."

Michael was exhausted but also quite anxious. He couldn't sit still, so he moved to the side of the raft closest to the riverside and dragged himself up onto the ground. He scrambled through the brambles and stumbled around, clearly in pain. It looked like he was having a panic attack, but all I could do was watch. He bent over, and I could tell that he was having problems with leg cramps. And to make it worse, the ground was peppered with sharp rocks that cut into his feet.

After a few minutes, he got his bearings and came back to the shore next to our boat.

"Have you seen anyone else?" Michael asked. I shook my head no.

Within minutes, Kevin, Thom's raft guide, floated into the water near the side of our boat. He pulled himself up on the ground next to Michael.

Greg arrived next and needed no help getting into the raft. He flipped up into the boat like a dolphin! It was crazy to watch. I went over to Greg and asked, "How did you jump up into the boat like that?"

He said, "The water was so cold, I didn't feel anything. I just jumped out and into the raft!"

Patrick appeared next. He shouted, "Yeah, someone give me a hand!" I helped him pull himself up and into the raft.

"I'm so glad to see you, Pat," Greg said.

Greg and Patrick lay on their backs in the back of my raft, looking at each other. They both started laughing. "Oh my God, that was wild," Patrick said.

I was delighted to see my nephews, knowing they were okay. But I had to take stock. We knew a couple of things: one, Thomas was in a different raft, so he was not thrown into the water. He was okay. But that left Thom and Nathan. The boys said they had both been thrown into the water on the other side of the raft. If either of them were injured or unconscious, they could have been caught in the current and carried downriver. Unable to signal for help, there was a high probability that they would be snagged in the buckbrush at the river's edge or in the branches of other foliage. That would mean that they wouldn't survive, and their bodies would not likely be found until the river receded in the future. Or worse yet, they would end up at the bottom of Pine Flat Lake, and we might never see them again.

The boys discussed that, while their biggest concern was their dad, since he was older and not quite as strong, they were also worried about Nathan. "Maybe they both made it to the riverbank and are trying to figure out how to get to us," Michael said.

We all nodded. I think that no one wanted to imagine losing them both.

To fight the fear, we took a deep breath. Patrick said, "We all need to scan the water. Maybe we should wade out into the water, holding hands, to form a chain so we can catch and pull them to the side when they come downstream."

"I have a rope," Kevin said.

"That's good!" Patrick said. "Oh my God, where the heck is Dad?"

We heard people calling out along the river, and no one else floated past. We were pretty confident that Thom must still be behind us, so I told them all that we needed to continue searching the waters for him.

Kevin had taken up a position in the front of the raft and secured the sixty-foot rope kept under the bow for rescues. Kevin had learned how to throw a coiled hose or rope in firefighting and basic EMT training.

"I've practiced throwing a coiled rope before, but haven't needed to use it for a rescue," Kevin said. "This is going to be challenging, but I'm on it."

Another raft came near us, moving just past our raft, and the men in it grasped branches of buckbrush to hold their position at the edge of the cove. We all scanned the water's surface and the brush.

"Wait! There's Dad!" Michael yelled.

Thom was floating downstream, face up. His arms were splayed out, his eyes and mouth wide open.

We all started yelling out his name. But he didn't respond.

"Why is he motionless?" Michael asked. "He looks dead. This is bad."

He was right. Nothing can prepare you for that scene. Nothing.

"Something's not right," Stacey said. "Why isn't he moving? Maybe he's hurt. If we're quick with the rope, we can snag him before he gets too far downstream."

Kevin already had the rope rolled so that it would unfurl as he threw it. "He's on his back, so if I throw the rope across his chest, maybe he can grab it, and we can pull him in. As the slack comes out and the rope slides across Thom's chest, he has to grab it quickly. He's still moving fast enough that there's only one chance this will work."

He made the sixty-foot throw with exceptional accuracy across Thom's chest.

We watched the rope fly through the air. Thom wasn't responding to anything, including our yelling, so we were afraid that he was either unconscious or he was gone.

I bellowed, "Thom, you have to grab that rope, brother!"

"Thom, grab the damn rope!" Kevin yelled.

"Dad, grab the rope. Dad, grab the rope," Greg said repeatedly.

"I think we're losing him," Patrick said. "He's not grabbing the rope. What will we do if he misses it?"

Stacey said, "The only way to get him will be to swim after him and rope him somehow so we can recover him. He's not responding, so he must be hurt. But his eyes are wide open!"

As the rope slid over his body, Thom suddenly reached up and grabbed it. When the rope became taut and we pulled on it, he submerged under the current. We collectively gasped, scanning the surface of the water for any sign of him.

He resurfaced near the bank of the river, not far from our raft. Michael, who was still on the riverbank beside our raft, stumbled over the rocks to get back into the water.

"I'm coming!" Michael yelled. He fell and quickly got back up. "My legs are still frozen!" But Michael pushed through and jumped into the water. He grabbed Thom's hand and held on tight to him, pulling him closer to the water's edge. "His eyes are glossed over." Michael's face looked grief-stricken.

We all scrambled out of the boat and onto the shore. Greg and Patrick landed first. "Michael, hand Dad to me and Patrick," Greg said. He and Patrick pulled Thom out and onto a tiny rocky area next to some shrubs. There was just enough room for him to lie there, but his legs were still partially in the water.

Michael tried to pry the rope from Thom's fingers. "I can't get him to let go of the rope!"

"He's not responding, and he's blue," Greg said. "We need to do CPR, Uncle Gordie!"

I knew CPR, but I never pictured myself in this kind of crisis. I was distraught. *Oh my God, what will I tell my mom? That her firstborn son was cradled in my arms, and I'm the one who should have done something about it, but couldn't?*

Because here's the ironic thing about this: people don't understand drowning. When you watch a movie and somebody has drowned, they bang them on the back, tilt their head down, and they cough and spit out water. In this case, it wasn't like that at all.

I checked his vitals, listening for a heartbeat and for any breath moving in his lungs. Nothing. Then I began CPR—chest compressions, and then rescue breaths. I also attempted to push on his stomach to get some water out of him. He was already very swollen. He did not respond, but I kept going.

Nathan suddenly arrived. Another raft had rescued him. He told Michael, "I got thrown out of our raft and grabbed at a rock after escaping the keeper, but I couldn't hold on to it. I was swept a bit further downstream and finally able to pull myself up on the riverside on the right. Not long afterward, another raft, coming downstream, saw me and pulled over. I was so relieved. They pulled me into their raft and brought me down to the left side here."

"Oh, man, Nate! I was worried about you," Michael said. The brothers hugged.

Nathan pointed to a raft two down from ours. "I was in that raft. When I got out, Nick looked over here where you are all standing and said. 'Don't go over there,' to me."

I said, "Of course, I'm going over there."

Nathan walked around the huddle of his brothers and, for the first time, realized that I was giving CPR to his dad. Nathan moaned. "It's Dad? Is he okay, Uncle Gordie? He doesn't look good. Why is he bluish? There's blood coming out of his mouth!"

I couldn't respond to Nathan. I was focusing on getting a response from Thom. I glanced up and saw that my son and nephews all looked so anxious and scared. I kept at CPR, picking up the pace, but there was no change.

"All that time, he's been underwater. I'm sure all that current went into his mouth, stomach, and lungs," Greg said.

All of a sudden, a bunch of stuff erupted out of his mouth that had been caught in his stomach. It was pretty graphic. Kevin, the guide, jumped in to help, but still, we couldn't get a heart or lung response.

My brother and one of my heroes, Gordon "Gordie" Miller—the one who began CPR on me.

Chapter 8
ETCHED IN OUR MINDS FOREVER
Saturday, May 27, 2006, 11:15 a.m.

Thomas's Perspective

I had been in a raft that had taken off later than the others, filled with strangers. When we got to the first big turn, I saw an empty raft trapped up against this big granite wall. I thought, "Oh my gosh, somebody's out of their boat." We angled out of it because we didn't want to run into that wall.

All the other boats were pulling up on the shore, some in a small bay and others a ways down. We pulled up alongside a long jetty-like strip of land. Getting out and up onto the ground, it was easy to pull the raft up where there wasn't any buckbrush. We all sat back down in the boat to rest. I could see a group of people up shore. Someone asked the guide what was happening, and he said they were probably trying to collect everyone who had been in the empty raft. I just sat there peacefully.

Stacey, another guide, came running up to our boat. She said she needed the first aid bag.

"Look, I was an Army medic," I explained. "I can go with you to help."

The two of us began jogging to the scene where she said CPR was in progress. "Who is the mask for and where is it?"

Stacey hesitated for just a moment. "An older man was pulled out of the water, and we're trying to resuscitate him. And our jog there is probably just another two hundred yards."

"Okay, let's go." It still didn't occur to me that it could be my dad.

We got to a manzanita bush, and I could hear my brother yelling at someone.

"Come on, Dad," Patrick shouted. "Come on!"

"It sounds like my dad is working on the resuscitation!" I said. But as I ran around the corner, I saw Dad lying on a rock and Uncle Gordie performing CPR on him.

I approached the scene. "What the heck?"

Uncle Gordie heard the alarm in my voice. "Thomas, he's unconscious with no vitals present. I've started CPR, compressions, and breathing. He's not breathing at all. His eyes are glazed and fixed. Kevin has been helping, and we've been switching places now and then between mouth-to-mouth and compressions. Some water is coming out of his mouth."

You could say I was stunned, but I was also ready to jump into action. I saw Dad and had the strangest thought. *Maybe if I just run backwards really fast, this will all go away.* It felt like a five-minute conversation with myself, but it was a split second.

I heard Michael say to our cousin Ben, "Hey, can we pray right now?"

Everybody who wasn't working on Dad got in a circle. "This is scary, and a quick prayer will help," Michael said.

I calmed myself and took over, while my brothers prayed. "Gordie, you did so well, thanks. But I can take this now. You know I'm well trained for it, and you've earned a rest."

"I'm right here if you need me," Gordie said.

"Okay, all right, let's go." I assessed the situation and got to work. The first thing for me when working with a patient is making sure my environment is right. When you come up on casualties, you usually take a second, maybe even longer, to get your bearings.

I was on my knees, thinking for about four seconds, five seconds, just really intense, and then said, "All right, this is what we're going to do. We'll grab him and take his wetsuit off as we carry him there." I pointed up to a flatter area with hard ground—not rock—just beyond where we were. "We're going to do CPR up there."

Michael, Gordie, Nathan, and Patrick carried Dad to this clearer area and laid him on his back.

"We're waiting for more instructions from you, Thomas," Patrick said. "What can we do?"

I just nodded, focused.

It had only taken one to two minutes to move Dad. I quickly checked his pulse and listened for breathing and/or chest rise, but there was none. And since he was so cold, I thought maybe I was missing something. I decided we would do CPR again and go from there. I started doing compressions and breaths. However, after five to seven minutes, I began to feel exhausted. I finally looked up and said, "Look, I need somebody to help me."

This big guy, Kevin, the guide of Dad's boat, said, "I'll help." He became a superhero.

I laid out the plan. "You're going to do breaths, and I'm going to do compressions because I have no breath left. I'm out of breath."

"Okay, okay," Kevin said.

He quickly jumped into position, and I started compressions; that's where I had to be very aggressive. I didn't care if I broke ribs. If I killed him this way, at least we would have done everything possible to prevent it. My whole goal was to try to touch the dirt on his backside.

Kevin and I were a good team. That man's breaths were gigantic. Dad's chest rise was out of this world. We continued for about ten to fifteen minutes.

At one point, it occurred to me that after all that time and compressions, no breath had happened, and it felt stale and uncomfortable. And I think people couldn't get past the thought that we were working on this dead body. I asked everyone to grab an extremity and start pushing blood back through his body. My brothers jumped in to help. Patrick grabbed an arm, Mike grabbed a leg, Nathan grabbed a leg, and Greg grabbed an arm. Others helped too. I didn't know if it would work, but it was worth a try.

Nathan suddenly stopped pushing on Dad's leg. He noticed that something was missing from this whole scene.

“Who has a phone on them that works up here?” Nathan yelled. Everyone shook their head. “What? No one has a working phone? I am pissed!” Nathan looked up to the sky, his face angry. “They should at least have one of those satellite phones!”

One of the guides asked if anyone could walk downriver until they got a signal to call 911. One of the rafters we didn’t know, Bill, volunteered to go. It was quite a hike—maybe fifteen or twenty miles. He left right away. He told us how it all came down when he returned.

According to Bill, he had been hiking for just a few minutes when a pickup coming downhill stopped. “I was surprised because our bus driver had told me he had never seen any traffic on that road coming downhill,” he said.

“‘Hey buddy, you look like you could use a ride!’ the driver said to me.

“He was an older man with a gray beard,” Bill said. “He’d been fishing that morning upriver and was headed home.

“I told him, ‘I’m with KRE, and we’ve just had a drowning; I’m desperate to get to where I can call 911.’”

“He calmly said, ‘That’ll be way down the road, closer to the lake. Jump in, and I’ll drive you. What happened? Did a raft flip?’

“‘Yeah,’ I told him. ‘We were having a great time, with plenty of whitewater. I didn’t see what happened, but it looked like they went over a rock and the raft flipped. The rapids where it happened are pretty intense today. They say nobody taking this trip has ever drowned. This is my first, but to have someone drown is scary. They’re doing CPR right now, and some people are praying, so we’re hopeful.’”

Bill told me that as they passed the wooden bridge that led to our campsite, the sign read, “Trimmer Springs Crossing,” identifying the part of the river they were on. After about thirty minutes, Bill finally got a signal on his phone, so he called 911. He said he hadn’t been expecting to make any calls, so he hadn’t charged his phone in a while—it was almost out of power.

Bill said that he told the operator succinctly what had happened, quickly, so his battery didn’t die before he finished. “I want to report a drowning, and we need a doctor. They're doing CPR right now, but it's pretty serious. We're just upriver from Trimmer Springs Crossing."

The operator told Bill, "We'll notify the medevac team and send an EMT emergency vehicle," and just then, his phone died.

The kind driver brought Bill back as close as he could get to where we were, and Bill hiked his way back to us.

We were all so grateful when he returned and told us help was on the way.

Greg's Perspective

While my brother, Thomas, and our guide, Kevin, were working on Dad, I was sure we would be able to save him. But by then, I began to have doubts. He'd been without vitals for a long time."

Patrick said to me, "Greg, we moved him a couple of minutes ago and got him onto the flat dirt, but he's still not coming around. Oh God! What if?"

Both of us could hear people crying, chatting, and whispering around us. Someone said, "He's gone."

Patrick asked, "Could we be witnessing our dad's death?" He became emotional, so overcome by such a terrible thought that it took him some time to compose himself. Then we were all crying. Patrick said, "Everybody's starting to sense the desperation that we are running out of time."

Patrick's eyes were misty with tears as he whispered to me, "Greg, our guide told me they're trained to do CPR for only about seven or eight minutes. After that, there's something like a ninety-nine percent chance that they're going to be brain-dead."

I shook my head, not able to even register that possibility.

"Look, Greg, they're walking away thinking this is their dad, so let them grieve here. But we're not quitting!"

I agreed. The brothers and Uncle Gordie were still trying to get movement and blood flow, and we would not stop. There was a lot of heavy breathing and intense, deep sobbing at the same time, and that desperation is well etched in our minds forever.

Everything Patrick was saying was in my heart as well. I was distraught. I was holding Dad's hand and saying, "Come back, Dad," which led me to pray over him. And right there by his side, all of a sudden, I looked around and saw everyone on their knees praying, which gave me some momentary relief, but it was short-lived. My mind was still wandering. *Oh crap. I don't think he's coming back.*

I got up and walked to this tree by a bush, out of the sight of everyone, and I fell on my knees and bawled. I said a meaningful prayer. "Father God, we need him here. Please don't take him. Send him back, I beg you, in Jesus's name."

Just then, some lady came up behind me and gently rubbed her fingers up and down on my back. I didn't know her, had never seen her before. She said, "It's going to be okay."

I said, "You know what? You're right. It is going to be okay." I had a sudden rush of peacefulness that relaxed me. I tried to look at her, but the sun was blinding me. I couldn't see her face.

It was strange because everyone at the CPR site had arrived in rafts and were wearing wetsuits. There wasn't anyone else there. No one else could have reached that spot along the river unless they had been in a boat, hiked a treacherous route, or flown there by helicopter. She was wearing a blue dress and nice shoes. When I turned around several seconds later, she was gone. No one else saw her that weekend, and she was never seen again.

I was mystified. That moment affected me.

"Hey, Greg," Patrick said when I approached my dad.

I nodded, grabbed Dad's right hand, and prayed again. They were still doing CPR, but when I finished the prayer, I saw this guy running toward us, shouting something I couldn't make out.

Thomas kept checking for a pulse. "I'm hoping to get a response," he said. "I feel that there is a calmness here, even though it has been too long to think he will make it. The biggest struggle is not being able to give an IV, and other things I know will help. I'm beginning to feel I've lost him."

Thomas spoke quietly out the side of his mouth to me. "Greg, how am I going to tell our brothers? Hey, sorry, guys. This isn't working. But what can we do but keep working on him?"

Just then, a man came running at us, holding something up. "Hey, I've got a CPR mask!"

It's one of those types that creates suction, making every breath highly effective. This was a boost to my faith that Dad would make it. It could make all the difference, and Thomas perked up!

Stacey spoke to the other rafters. "This CPR effort will likely take a while, and we have all the help we need. We hope a helicopter arrives soon, but there's no sense in hanging around here. Climb back in your rafts and go back to the campsite." About ten rafts were loaded up to return to KRE.

Thomas told me that one problem with chest compressions is that the lungs naturally act like a balloon, so the larynx makes noise, and you don't know whether the person is moaning or it's just air escaping from the lungs.

As we all watched, Thomas rechecked Dad's pulse to see if he was making the noise and then started to resume compressions. "Wait! I just felt it—a thwack under my hand on his chest!" Thomas said. Hope was revived. "Now it's gone again. Wait! Now it's back!"

And suddenly Dad moved, very poltergeist-ish—chest forward, head back.

Thomas pushed Dad onto his side and started pounding on his back. Water and blood were coming out.

One second later, Dad tried to get up. He lifted his chest and coughed.

"Let's sit him up," Thomas said.

So Patrick, Nathan, and I lifted him into a sitting position. And Dad said something in Vietnamese! "Choi oi." I've heard him say it a million times—it means "Good grief!" It seemed odd in this scene, but to me it meant that he is here and might not have brain damage.

Michael got up, freaked out for a minute, and then came back. "You know, Greg, everything can change in one moment," he said. "But we all know we still need that helicopter to find us."

I still wondered whether Dad's "choi oi" was a good sign. I asked him, "Did you smoke some bad pot?" And he let out a little chuckle. And I was like, all right, his cognitive function is still there! *Oh my God, I got my dad back*!

My brother Nathan is a personal injury attorney, so he sees drownings and similar situations often, and the brain damage that follows. He said to us all, "At this point, I think we all are saying that he is alive and his brain seems to be functioning!"

I saw Kevin get up close to my dad and ask, "Thom, are you doing okay?"

He didn't respond right away. He had no idea what had happened. A few minutes later, he mumbled something about needing to stand, probably just some significant anxiety manifesting itself.

"Hey, somebody help me stand up so I can walk it off," Dad said as he gasped. But he didn't have the strength to stand. We moved him over a few feet to a tree so he could sit up leaning against it.

Thomas said, "Baloney, Dad. You're not walking this off! Sit up, stay still, breathe deeply, and relax. With a little luck, the 911 helicopter will be on the way soon."

We were all having a conversation with him and each other. "This is so weird," Nathan said. "Seriously, he just died!" Nathan expounded on how miraculous it seemed to all of us there. "He's saying, 'I'm not going anywhere.' We're all thinking, 'You were just dead, and now you've come back! We're celebrating!'"

We sat there for about an hour and a half. We knew the helicopter was coming because at some point, Bill returned and told us he'd made the 911 call. Fairly often, Thomas asked Dad how he was doing. "Dad, are you okay? What do you need?" Dad just said he was good.

Thomas was evaluating the situation. "We've got the helicopter coming. But we have no idea how or when it will come. How will it find us? Hey, I've got an idea! Let's use several of the life vests to create a circle with them out in the field next to us! That's just how I would have done it in an Army evac situation." We all agreed, and while Patrick, Michael, and I stayed with Dad, the others created the life vest landing zone!

Dad's breathing, although extremely shallow, was enough for him to maintain limited consciousness, but he could barely talk. He was slurring words, not focused, and sometimes not even making sense.

The only spot on that whole five-mile stretch of the river where a helicopter could land was right where we happened to pull my dad out of the water. It was almost as if we all needed to have this experience. It was like God saying, "Hey, I'm going to use your dad to teach you guys that I'm real." After that experience, I would never question my faith again. That's my story.

The helicopter that flew me to University Medical Center in Fresno, California (now named Community Regional Medical Center). This spot was the only clearing large enough for landing this chopper, and it was close to where my son was administering CPR to me.

Chapter 9
PILLSBURY DOUGHBOY
Saturday, May 27, 2006, Noon

Kelly's Perspective

Much of the following was shared with me by my sons, my brother-in-law, and others involved with the drowning. I was blissfully unaware of what was happening to my husband, Thom, but I occasionally thought of him and my sons up on the King's River that day. I would soon learn a lot about drownings, recoveries, lifesaving measures, and caring for someone in the aftermath of drowning.

The CHP helicopter, a two-seater with a small space where a back seat could be arranged, was uneventfully patrolling the highways over Sanger, California, and listening to the frantic communications from the 911 chopper as they desperately searched for my husband and boys near Trimmer Springs. Andrea Brown, the CHP EMT, thought they might be on the Kings River, so she and her pilot, Paul Dwyer, decided to cruise over Pine Flat and up the Kings to look for them.

They had seen several EMT vehicles dispatched from Fresno enroute to Pine Flat Lake and knew that even if they could find them, it would be several hours before they would arrive. Probably way too late for lifesaving efforts. They were highly experienced in search and rescue and recovery operations, having been well-decorated for many years of service, and this wasn't their first rodeo.

Andrea told me about the conversation she had in the helicopter at that moment. "Paul, if this happened while they were rafting, they are most likely to be on the Kings River in the Canyon," she said to the pilot. "Why don't we cruise up the Kings and see if we can find them? I don't see Trimmer Springs being their location." It was just a short diversion to cruise over Pine Flat Lake and then up the river, so Paul called in his intent to search up the Kings. Once they entered the

Canyon, after crossing Pine Flat Lake, they would be out of communication and off the grid. CHP approved, so they proceeded.

The place where Kevin and Michael had pulled Thom out of the water, on the edge of the river, had a patch of flat ground that had been a sandbar when the water was lower—it had no buckbrush on it and no trees nearby. It turned out that the sandbar was the only place within several miles where a helicopter could land—there were no other open areas anywhere. Trees on both ends of it and the Canyon wall next to it, and surrounded by buckbrush too high to land in, made that sandbar like an oasis in a desert—no other options, placed perfectly for an extraction like only this CHP crew could execute.

They found my family within ten minutes of cruising up the river and zeroed in on the life jacket landing zone that the rafters had made. Flying in the Kings Canyon is usually pretty tricky, with winds gusting from all directions, but Paul nailed the landing. Because most of the Canyon is so deep and narrow, with granite on both sides and varying foliage as elevations fluctuate, air temperatures change quickly as the sun's elevation shifts. This causes windy conditions, which are very difficult to anticipate.

It was around 12:15 p.m. on this eventful Saturday when the gang on the ground heard the helicopter approaching and then landing. My boys told me how they were overwhelmed with emotion—even Thom, having one of his moments of consciousness, and experiencing the feeling of being in Vietnam again. He said it was a "powerful sense of 'here comes the cavalry!'" Still struggling to breathe, he had a sense of relief and gratitude.

The helicopter landed, and Andrea Brown jumped out and went over to the boys, thinking they were recovering a dead body. They were surprised that Thom was alive and breathing—barely.

Andrea said, "We've got to put him on a backboard and into the chopper."

When Andrea and Paul brought out a stretcher, she immediately put a neck brace on Thom and hooked him up to an IV, then loaded him onto it.

"He's going to be fine," she said to the boys.

Our boys and the other campers were excited and rejoicing, glad that Thom had overcome the hump and would soon be headed to the hospital.

Once Thom was stabilized on the stretcher, Paul and Andrea had the boys load him into the left side of the helicopter, with his feet under the dash. They lifted off for the twenty-minute flight to the University Medical Center in Fresno. It had one of the few Level One Trauma Centers on the West Coast.

Andrea watched Thom closely as they flew.

Suddenly, Thom gasped, "I can't breathe … I need air …" then he passed out. His heart stopped. Andrea administered lidocaine through his IV to get his heart going, and it worked.

The boys began their trek back to the cars and down to the hospital. First, they had to return to their rafts to reach the camp. They told me later that it was not easy for them to be on a raft after what had happened.

"Someone asked if we wanted to float down the river, as we could get to Fresno faster, or get in the trucks and drive down," Thomas said. "And I thought, yeah, let's get on a raft and go. But my brothers are like, hell no, I'm not getting on a boat again. I understood. But we did have to get in the raft to get to the camp."

Michael was not pleased with the idea, but there was no other way. "I'll never forget getting back down the river, and then not even having an oar or paddle," he said. "That was nerve-wracking. Yeah, it was somebody else's raft. Now you have this big guy in a full raft without a paddle. I'm dead weight. And I was freaking out the entire trip. I would say it was an hour, an hour and a half, until we got off the raft, and I was freaking out the whole time. I don't know if anybody knew it, but I was having a panic attack inside. And then going through the first rapid; yeah, I wanted to say, I'll walk back."

"Once back at the camp, we started collecting all of our stuff, just throwing it in the truck," Thomas said. "It was like not even packing.

We drove right to the hospital. And we didn't get a cell signal for a while. We felt like, wow, we did this. You know, all is good. Dad's in the hospital already, and healing up. We're saying things like, holy crap, that was crazy. Wow, we did it."

Of course, my boys' perspectives were limited once my husband was on the helicopter. They could only try to get to the hospital as quickly as possible.

As the helicopter approached Fresno, Paul called the Highway Patrol office and had them contact me to inform me of what had happened.

I was shopping with Elizabeth at the time.

"Oh my goodness, Mom, you just commented about the river and how it was so full," Elizabeth said. "You even said you hoped they were okay. And now we get this call from the CHP, just a moment later?" My hazel-eyed girl was flabbergasted and tearing up—I could tell she was trying not to panic.

Yes, it was odd that we had just been talking about them when the CHP called me. The dispatch person said that Thom had been in a serious rafting accident and was being flown to the ER at UMC, which is University Medical Center. They suggested I get there as soon as possible. Elizabeth and I knew it had to be serious for a CHP officer to call because it meant that Thom couldn't communicate with us himself. And because he was airlifted, we knew it must not be good news.

I had no contact with the boys for a while, until they got further down from the mountains. And they thought everything was fine. I called Tim, who hadn't gone rafting with the others, and he showed up at the hospital not long after we did.

I reached Thomas, who was driving down from the river, to let the boys know where I was.

"Thomas, Dad's not doing well."

"Wait, what? What are you talking about? Who screwed this up? We got a pulse. He talked. What could be wrong?"

I was overwhelmed, so Tim got on the phone. "Dad coded twice in the helicopter."

"Are you talking about the same guy?" Thomas asked.

"Just get here as soon as you can."

When the helicopter carrying Thom landed at the UMC helipad, which is near the ER entrance, the crash crew immediately loaded him onto a gurney and took him into the ER. An auto accident victim had just come in, badly injured, and the triage nurse was processing him when they brought Thom in. Annette was typically an ICU (intensive care) nurse, but was sitting in for a friend that day. She took one look at Thom and recognized that minutes were critical. She had them begin measures to stabilize him, getting him ready for the only bed they had in the ICU, because she could see the effects of severe acidosis setting in.

When the body's need for oxygen exceeds the supply, acids build up in the blood, and the pH drops precipitously. The kidneys must then strike a balance by removing excess water and acid. If this doesn't happen, tissues begin to swell. Thom's body began swelling, and his finger was turning purple because of his wedding ring. He was starting to resemble the Pillsbury Doughboy, quickly becoming unrecognizable. The swelling would stop, and tissues would return to normal when enough oxygen began to reach the blood.

I was told these things, but I still wasn't allowed to see him. Internally, I struggled to keep my imagination in check. I knew that I needed to be strong for my family.

At that point, Thom was barely aware of anything, still scarcely awake, wondering what they were going to do next. He wasn't even mindful that he wasn't wearing any clothes because when they did CPR on him, they stripped off his wetsuit, leaving him in his underpants.

"I'm going to move this patient in ahead of the car accident because he's showing signs of severe damage from acidosis, which will get worse very quickly," Annette said to the charge nurse. "I need him prepped, STAT, for a central line and intubation. We have one bed in the ICU, and that's where he's headed next. Dr. Javed will be here shortly and will take care of it."

Annette looked over Thom's body once more. "I also need an orderly to bring a metal cutting tool to remove his wedding ring. Look, his finger's turning purple!"

"I've got it, Annette. It'll be easy," Bob said. He was part of the crash crew that took Thom off the helicopter. "I'll put it in his special effects bag when his kids bring his clothes in. He didn't have any clothes when he arrived, only underwear, and they're in the laundry now."

They kept Thom in the ER as they attempted to stabilize him—blood gases were haywire, breathing extremely shallow and intermittent, BP very low and fluctuating, etc. At this point, they administered a sedative, which knocked him out, because most of the protocol from here on would be invasive with tubes and hoses for delivery into his bloodstream.

Finally, he was taken to the ICU, where they prepped him for the ventilator, installed tubes via his throat to provide air for his lungs, and pumped him with a respirator, which had to be adjusted constantly to keep from blowing his lungs up. They put a "central line" in Thom's chest to deliver drugs immediately into the bloodstream and set him up for a powerful regimen of procedures, which are defined in the "standard of care" for cases like this, or so I'm told.

Elizabeth and I, along with Tim, were ushered into "the quiet room," a small, private area usually reserved for those who will be receiving some bad news. I was highly apprehensive about that, having been there after my sister and her husband were in a head-on motorcycle crash in 2001 and in that very same ICU.

This photo, taken looking upstream, reveals the rock where the keeper developed.

This photo shows some of Bonzai.

You can see from this diagram where I was pulled out of the water and onto the rocky area, where Gordie began CPR. Also visible is the tree-covered area where the boys moved my body to enable Thomas to continue CPR. And the helicopter landed where the broken line is at the top. Stacey Serra took and identified these three photos for me while I was hospitalized.

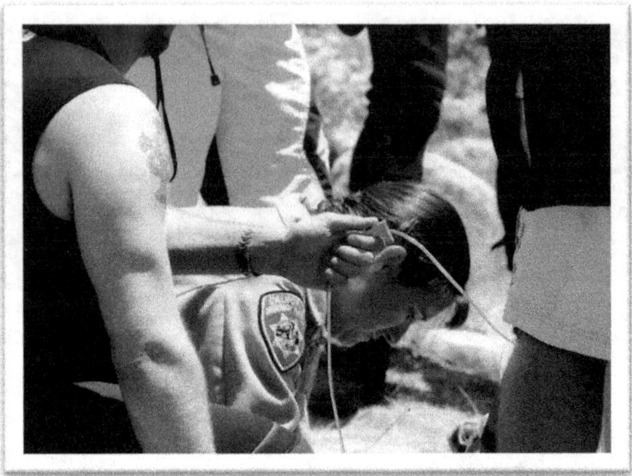

EMT Andrea Brown is on the ground at the spot where I had been waiting for the helicopter, placing my IV. My son, Thomas, is holding the IV bag.

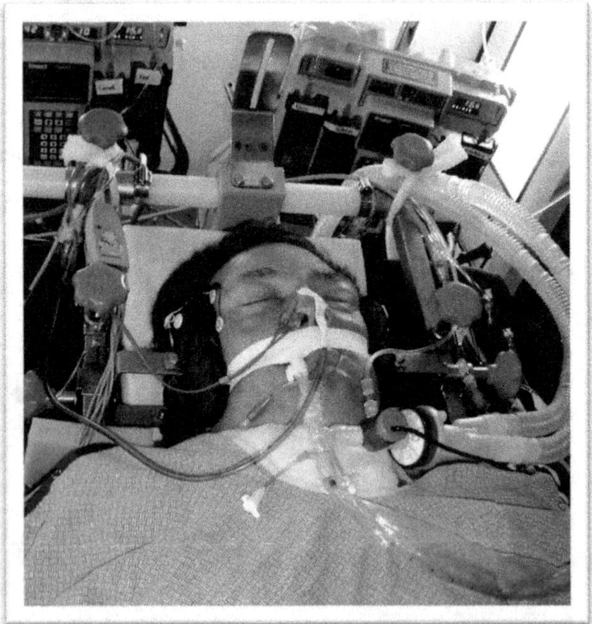

As is common for revived drowning victims, I swelled up like the Pillsbury Doughboy. In this photo, I was in an induced coma and hooked up to a ventilator and affixed to the Roto-Rest bed.

Chapter 10
THE QUIET ROOM
Saturday, May 27, 2006, Mid-Afternoon

Kelly's Perspective

Tim, Elizabeth, and I waited in the quiet room for the doctors to give us more information. We were told they would come and speak to us when the doctor had stabilized him, so we sat there, very uncomfortably worried, but dealing with it together.

Most people think, "Oh, he drowned, but he was resuscitated. He'll be okay." But that wasn't the case. When the doctor finally approached, he said anything but that.

"This is a severe injury," Dr. Usman Javed said. "And, since he's an insulin-dependent diabetic, it's going to be a while."

Tim couldn't go rafting because he had injured his right knee—specifically a tear to the MCL—and he was sorry to have missed it. However, at this point, he was glad he hadn't gone.

"You know, Mom, even before attending nursing school, I was the most medically astute of the whole crew," Tim said. "And so, now that this has happened, I can be here for you, Mom. I'm here to relay important information to the physicians—things about Dad they don't know—and to keep all of you informed and up to date. I can lead you through and around all this. And I can advocate for you and Dad. You're really stoic, Mom, but you also need help."

"I agree, Tim. I really do need you."

"I think God had a plan," Tim said. "I'm not traumatized from the river experience because I wasn't there. Remember, I was a lifeguard and could have performed CPR, but so could the others there, and they did. So I think it's more important for me to be here with you."

Tim was right. He was just what I needed to help me navigate all this medical jargon and the decisions to be made. When he turned his kind brown eyes to me, I knew he would tell me the truth.

“How soon can we go see him?” I asked Dr. Javed.

“There are a lot of considerations, not the least of which is that we are working overtime to stabilize his metrics,” the doctor said. “Many things we’re working on all at once, so we’re busy. When he’s more under control, we’ll let you visit. He’s unconscious right now, and we’re putting him in a coma while he’s on the RotoRest bed. He’s intubated with a respirator, doing his breathing. We’ll keep him in the ICU until we can remove the respirator and take him off the RotoRest. How long that will be depends on the changes in his metrics.”

“What’s that?” Elizabeth asked.

“The metrics are your dad’s neurological function and respiratory status,” Dr. Javed explained. “The X-rays we’ve taken show that his lungs are filled with water; it’s what we call a ‘whiteout.’ The alveoli in the lungs are highly sensitive tissues, and the water within them is slightly acidic. The acid causes the tissue to harden and eventually scar. Once scarring develops, his breathing will be impaired permanently and indefinitely. To prevent scarring, which occurs when water stagnates, we fasten him to a slowly rolling, constantly moving bed to keep the water in motion. Eventually, excess water is absorbed and removed by the kidneys; since he has diabetes, his kidney function could be deteriorating. We’re watching that too.

“At this point, his diagnosis is ‘acute respiratory distress syndrome,’ ARDS, and we have a protocol to follow to ensure the best results. No one knows whether he’s got brain injuries because he was without oxygen for at least twenty-five minutes. We’re hopeful he’ll pull through, but the odds that he’ll return to normal again are pretty poor.”

Tim interpreted. “Dr. Javed is suggesting that if Dad does recover, he could have trouble breathing for the rest of his life, and his activity level could be limited by his ability to process oxygen. Not a very positive picture. But they are watching his numbers, such as those on the pulse oximeter, arterial blood gases, and respiratory rate.”

It was difficult for me to accept all this. I needed to see Thom.

When they stabilized him, they took me to his ICU bed, but he was not conscious. Still, I held his hand for just a little bit. And then they ushered me out. He was swollen, and a lot was going on with him—IVs and tubes, and he didn't look good. And he was not responsive to me. He wasn't aware. It was great that I got to stand next to him for a little while, though. I was hopeful because he was alive, but you know, when you don't know what you don't know, you don't see how scared or sad you should be. I mean, I knew just by looking at him that there was a possibility of death.

I don't think they wanted to pull any punches with me. They didn't with my brother-in-law and my sister after their accident, either. They told us about the horrible injuries they both had suffered, and they were saying, if they make it through the night, we're on a good trajectory. But with Thom, it was different; if he makes it through forty nights and days, maybe he'll be okay. They tell you like it is.

"All this debris from the river is in his lungs," Tim explained. "And so, you know, typically, what happens when your lungs have something foreign inside of them, they create these little granulomas. They take calcium and wall off the infected areas. However, that's a long-term, not a short-term, solution. He has extensive lung inflammation due to the presence of foreign bodies, including contaminated river water and sand. As a result, his body is inflamed. When tissue inflammation occurs, it swells and starts to leak fluid. And that leaking of fluid creates more fluid, and you've got to figure out how to drain that. Similar to pneumonia."

Thom's brother, Larry, was a respiratory tech, and he taught respiratory technology. When he arrived at the hospital, he walked back to see Thom and the technician. Thomas went with him and told me all about it when Larry left.

"Mom, Uncle Larry asked them what they were using on Dad," Thomas said. "There was one thing that he told them they didn't need to be using on him. The technician showed him what it did. He knew about it, but hadn't seen it used before. That trauma unit was top-notch. Uncle Larry was, I wouldn't say pessimistic, but he was very straightforward about Dad's condition. 'He's in bad shape, so he might not come out of this.'"

It was challenging to explain my shock to my kids. "I thought you could lay him down on a downward-angled board and the water would slowly flow out of his lungs," I said. "I was horrified when they told me that the water must be absorbed by the body, processed by the kidneys, and excreted as urine." The whole process could take a month or more. And that's providing their dad lives that long, given all the other things going wrong.

At this time, I officially appointed Tim as the family's "spokesman," even though he had already been serving in that role. He would interface with the doctors, keep the family updated on Thom's progress, and relay the family's concerns to them.

Later in the day, Dr. Javed explained that the standard of care called for a tracheotomy, but Tim refused it. He didn't believe that it was necessary. After all, he had seen his dad talking while the helicopter was searching for them. Dr. Javed had a call and left the room. Tim would wait to share his concerns with the doctor until they were alone. With his dad now intubated and out like a light, he decided to let him rest and went back to the waiting room, where he sat with me and a resident. Tim didn't have to wait long.

Dr. Javed was on the trauma team doing his residency, so he was all over the ICU. Understanding our arrangement, he pulled Tim back into a hallway to talk to him and an intern again. Once again, Tim relayed what he learned to me. It went like this:

"You know, we put your dad in a coma now," Dr. Javed said. "But from what he went through, it doesn't sound like he will make it. And I don't think you necessarily want him to make it. We want to discuss withdrawing care. He was dead for a long time, and he most likely suffered significant brain damage."

"I'm astounded," Tim said. "Hey, no, he was awake! He was talking before they got him on the helicopter. I spoke to one of my brothers, who talked with him on the scene while waiting for the helicopter to arrive."

"What are you talking about?" the doctor asked.

"He woke up after CPR, and they put him on the helicopter. He was talking before he was on the helicopter. I think he even talked to the medic on it."

The two doctors looked at each other in bewilderment. They were shocked that he had been talking. "Well, that changes everything," Dr. Javed said. "We'll do all we can to bring him back to health."

Tim was enjoying being the liaison between the family and the physicians and took the position seriously—and it's a good thing. I'm so glad he was able to tell Dr. Javed that vital information before they gave up on Thom!

Tim's Perspective

As the liaison between the doctors and our family, I was busy in those first few days of Dad's hospitalization. It was up and down, moment by moment.

Back on the second day in the trauma ICU, I remember the cardio team coming out and saying, "Hey, what's his cardiac history?"

I told them he had no cardiac history, as far as we know.

They said, "Well, you know, his ejection fraction is fifteen or twenty percent." That was super low. You need to be over fifty percent to be walking around. And they were shocked that his number was that low and that we hadn't had any prior problems with him related to his heart.

Your lungs and your heart are connected, so the injury to his lungs was so severe that it stressed out his heart, and now he wasn't getting a good blood flow from his lungs to his heart. Your blood returns to your heart from your body, and then it's pumped to the lungs. From there, it's back to the heart and then circulated throughout the body after being oxygenated by the heart. And because his lungs were so traumatized, it affected his cardiac output and caused low blood pressure, so Dad was in severe distress.

They were planning to do a Swan-Ganz catheter right then. That means they were going to stick a balloon catheter into Dad's heart to measure the pressures to try to figure out what was going on. It was a fairly standard procedure, but also somewhat risky. We discussed it with them and gave our consent to proceed. It's a sterile procedure, and they were at his bedside, ready to do it. Right before they were going to start cutting him to put a guide wire in to insert the catheter, his heart rate suddenly changed. His blood pressure went up just like that!

We had asked everyone in the waiting room to pray that he wouldn't need the catheter, and he didn't!

Using the central line that had been installed in Dad's chest, they began delivering drugs for various issues, including fentanyl, blood thinners, more blood pressure regulators, Versed, a hypnotic, a paralytic, antibiotics, and other pharmaceutical tools. Truly a pharmacopeia.

The doctors were all a little surprised that Dad had no broken ribs after all that CPR. Usually, desperate CPR breaks ribs, but not his. I credit this to the excellent work of Gordie, Thomas, and Kevin. It was as if they practiced CPR every day, although they didn't. He was bruised, but not severely, and it didn't inhibit the recovery measures the hospital employed.

With the tubes down his throat and the drugs to keep him from moving, Dad couldn't voluntarily move any part of his body—we were glad he was unconscious because that would have upset him a great deal.

We all spent a lot of time in the waiting room. My sister Elizabeth described us best. "We have a huge family, right, Tim? And when we have traumatic things like this, we all come together. Think of the times we've done this."

She was right. We were hanging out together, reminiscing, and chatting. We took over the waiting room and stayed there day and night. Elizabeth bought a TV and brought it to the waiting room so that we could watch movies.

"It's hard because we can see him, but we aren't getting much feedback from him, Tim," Elizabeth said. "I hate that he's in a coma.

"Still, thank you, Tim, for being so good at explaining what's going on," she said kindly. "Every day is a roller coaster, and it's hard wondering if he will live. He could have some brain damage."

I nodded. She was right, and no matter what, he was going to have a long and challenging recovery.

For close to three weeks, Dad was kept unconscious on the RotoRest bed, constantly rolling side to side. During that time, he was unaware, having been fed a liquid diet through a feeding tube.

One consequence of the drugs that Dad was given was that he developed a "stress (bleeding) ulcer." On June 10th, using special endoscopic equipment, the doctor was able to go into his stomach, alongside the endotracheal tube, to cauterize the ulcer. If he hadn't still been intubated, the process would have been much more complicated, but it went smoothly. He was given a pint of blood to make up for what he had lost.

My grandmother, who was influential in the multi-level marketing industry, was a Mannatech distributor and had introduced Dad to one of their products, Ambrotose, several years earlier. It was a powdered stabilized derivative of aloe. Aloe vera had a half-life of twenty minutes after separation from the plant, but this product had a longer shelf life. It contained seven powerful, essential sugars, along with a proprietary blend of other healthy ingredients.

Grandma, who was with us at the hospital off and on, thought he should be taking Ambrotose through his feeding tube, as it was considered a powerful healing agent and is said to be a factor in repairing neural connections. The doctors, with a "Well, it can't hurt anything" attitude, finally agreed to allow it. I don't think it was an FDA-approved product and wasn't prescribed for any conditions. Typically, any products outside of the "standard of care" aren't allowed, as if something goes wrong, the hospital could face liability. However, in Dad's case, truth be told, nobody knew if the hospital protocol would work at all.

Starting a couple of days after treatment began, they started feeding Dad a hefty dose of Ambrotose—a tablespoon is a large dose—mixed with diet Sprite, in his feeding tube about every four hours during the day. It had to be combined with something it would dissolve in, since it's a dehydrated powder and could have clogged the feeding tube. One of the nurses refused, thinking the "sugars" would wreak havoc with Dad's diabetes, but when she wasn't there, everyone else cooperated. The product had no sweetness and did not affect blood sugar levels. I found it disconcerting that so many medical professionals had opinions about Ambrotose without having any knowledge of what it was or what it did. My grandmother was a stalwart, with a pleasant disposition and a firm sense of correctness—she insisted it be part of Dad's diet, and finally, the doctors approved.

We were beginning to see improvements in Dad and were looking forward to more of that. I do know that being together is what helped us all get through this time of uncertainty.

In the ICU waiting room, Tim, Kevin, Jeb, Patrick, Nick, Kelly, Greg, Thomas, Elizabeth, Nathan, and Michael; Kelly is holding the oar that everyone at KRE signed for me. It still hangs on a wall in my home today.

KRE owners Jeb and Julie at the hospital ER waiting with my family.

Our raft guide, Kevin, signing the "diary" the family created for me while they spent all those days in the ICU waiting room.

Chapter 11
WHAT HAS BEFALLEN ME?
Thursday, June 15, 2006, 3:00 a.m.

Thom's Perspective

They slowly began withdrawing the hypnotics on Wednesday evening, June 14th, after I had been moved to a regular bed. When I first came to, it must have been sometime in the wee hours of June 15th. It was quiet all around me; nobody was talking, just the usual sounds of hospital machines, especially the respirator at the head of my bed. I was utterly helpless, unable to move any part of my body—not even my little finger. I couldn't turn my head to see what time it was on the clock at the nursing station to my left.

Looking at the white tiles on the ceiling, I suddenly visualized a video playing. I was looking down at a rushing river from about thirty feet above, watching the water in all its power as it created what we call whitewater. I saw what looked like a keeper. It looked like water was being pumped up and down, causing occasional rolling on the surface that curled inward. There was no sound, but amazing, bright colors and distinct clarity, and a shining light from behind me—like a searchlight—illuminating the river below me. The portion of the river I was watching was a crashing, turbulent stretch of rapids, swift-moving and intense. Watching the rapids was mesmerizing, as they constantly changed and looked ominous. I was completely calm and focused as I watched this stunningly beautiful scene. Then the video faded to gray and stopped. I had never had an experience like this video before—I later likened it to what one might experience with LSD, but I didn't have any LSD!

Suddenly, I was flooded with the traumatic memory of what had happened. I remembered being caught in the keeper and reaching for the surface when I was pulled down before I could get a breath. I wasn't panicking, although the memory of fighting off drowning was vexing. My heart was pounding, and my head felt tight. I just needed answers, and wished I could talk to someone—anyone.

Did I die? How did I end up at this hospital? Where am I, and why am I all alone? Why are these tubes in my throat?

Mechanical breathing was facilitated by the machine positioned just behind my bed. No one was to be seen anywhere. But I couldn't even turn my head; I couldn't be sure of anything. *Was I in an accident, and am I now paralyzed?* There was something more teasing the back of my mind, and I thought I might remember something, but then it went blank again.

A nurse finally came and checked on me and was surprised to find me looking around and in a state of apparent confusion and consternation. She didn't expect me to have revived so soon, so she gently told me the details: I was in the ICU at UMC and had been sedated for almost three weeks while I was affixed to the RotoRest bed. They had just moved me to a regular bed this morning; several expert doctors had been tweaking my respirator to increase my PEEP score.

I had no idea what that was, but I later found out it stands for Positive End-Expiratory Pressure, which measures the force with which the lungs can exhale. A higher number indicates that the alveoli collapsed during exhalation, thereby increasing the volume of air exchanged with the blood. I had finally gotten to the point where they were ready to move me up a notch. But she explained that removing the ventilator prematurely is a no-no because putting it back in is highly traumatic.

It turns out that I had awakened around 3:00 a.m., and the nurse spoke to me about two hours later. Kelly came in to see me around 6:00 a.m., after the nurse had informed her that I was awake. She explained that there were about fifty friends and family cycling through the waiting room, many maintaining an all-night vigil, never knowing when I would finally be revived from the hypnotics and would be back in the land of the living. These wonderful people had taken over the waiting room, and they'd be excited to know I was finally awake!

“Thom, you’ve been in a rafting accident, and you’re in the hospital.” Kelly spoke to me very slowly and deliberately, stressing each word as if she didn’t believe I’d be able to understand.

Aw, really? I’ll bet you guys think I’m brain-dead! I can't even move my lips or utter a sound, so I hope this condition resolves! She had no way of knowing what was going on in my head. I will confess that I was glad to see her and hear that I would get to see some of the family soon.

“Dad’s finally awakened; he’s intubated and can’t move,” Kelly told the family. “But I’m going to keep going in and telling him, ‘We're having a party out in the waiting room. We miss you, but I want you to know we are partying out there, and you're invited.’”

Son Nathan was one of the first of my children to see me after I awoke from the induced coma. “Hi Dad, can you hear me?” he asked.

I could, but I was hooked up to the respirator still and couldn’t respond in any way.

“Why are you looking at the window, Dad?”

I was looking at Nathan, then at the window, then back and forth.

“Are you trying to tell me something?”

I was very frustrated, mainly because my hands were tied down. I couldn’t even gesture to him. I wanted to tell him to open the window and throw the TV out! I wasn’t about to lie in that bed and do nothing but watch television. But I couldn’t express it. He seemed sad that he couldn't understand what I wanted or needed.

This whole thing with paralysis, weakness, tubes, and hoses was going to get unbearable if I couldn’t find some light at the end of the tunnel. I felt so out of control.

It reminded me of another time in my life when I felt I had lost complete control. I thought about my old Cessna TU206F.

Flashback: What Just Happened? 1979

In 1979, my young insulation company had an office in Redding, which was thriving at the time. Driving up from Fresno took more than six hours one-way and was arduous. But I had to do it because it was essential for me to be at that office at least every two weeks.

I decided to look for an airplane to buy. I met a contractor who had one and wanted to sell it because he was retiring, so I purchased his Cessna TU206F—turbocharged, with oxygen, and loaded with instruments. Immediately, I set about to learn to fly! The plane had six seats and was a lovely aircraft. As a student, you are required to spend "dual time" with another licensed pilot, which my instructor thought would be him, but my brother, Jim, was also a pilot. He flew with me to complete the task efficiently, saving me a significant amount of money. After I got my license, which took about six months, I would fly up to Redding for sales meetings and general management functions about three times a month. The flight would take about an hour and a half each way. And it was fun!

One day, flying back to Fresno in the early evening, I had my sales manager, Eric Lofton, with me. As usual, while flying over the Bay Area, I checked in with "Bay Approach" to advise them that I was passing through and asked them to inform me of any nearby traffic—something they do regularly.

"Bay approach, this is Station-air November niner five two seven golf, heading to Fresno, requesting traffic advisories."

"Two seven golf, squawk four two one two."

I entered it into my transponder. "Two seven golf, four two one two."

"Two seven golf, we have your location. Be advised that you have no traffic nearby. It's a quiet evening here. We'll keep you apprised."

"Affirm, thanks, two seven golf out."

We were at about 10,500 feet, cruising smoothly at 140 knots, and watching the sun start to set over the Golden Gate. It was a beautiful sight. All was well in our world. But somehow, I was bored!

"Eric, how long do you think it'd take the DME to recalculate our ground speed if I changed the metrics on it quickly?" I had my DME (distance-measuring equipment) set to a radio frequency in Fresno. It would create a hypothetical right triangle, using my altitude as the base leg, the hypotenuse as the distance to the transmitter in Fresno, and then recalculate the other leg as the ground speed. It's an analog instrument, as were all of them then, and I was curious how quickly it would respond to a sudden change in altitude, changing the base leg abruptly. Could it recalculate fast?

"I'll bet it wouldn't take more than five seconds," Eric said. "What do you have in mind?"

Without telling Eric what I was doing, I quickly slammed my wheel forward, and we went into a steep dive. Instantaneously, we were rocked by a huge roar and gust of wind as a twin Piper went over us, right at the same level where we had been. It had been approaching from my left wing and was behind the wing. We would never have seen what hit us. I'm sure he was on autopilot, and Eric and I, white as sheets, watched as he continued toward San Francisco.

"What just happened?" Eric was completely awestruck. I was too. Freaked out would be a better description.

"Somehow, we've been spared an awful end," I said. "That guy was probably going three hundred and level with us, and we were so busy looking on our right, enjoying the view of the Golden Gate, that I didn't see him on my left. Eric, the explosion would have blown us into such small pieces that we'd have had a funeral with empty caskets!

"We're almost out of Bay Approach's area, so I assume they thought we were already talking to Castle." We would ask Castle Approach for advisories, too, as we went over Castle Air Base. Usually, I would have called Bay Approach and reported the event, and someone would have been reprimanded; however, Eric and I were in a state of shock. I didn't call them.

We prayed for a few moments as we tried to regain our composure. Clearly, the urge to check my DME's performance was not my idea, but was planted by God! It was just too off-the-wall, unusual, and extraordinary. I still get goosebumps relating to this. It feels like it happened yesterday.

The rest of the trip was uneventful. We landed in Modesto, where Eric lived, and when I dropped him off, we were both still shaken. Then, I went on to Fresno. I mentioned the experience, casually, to my wife, making it sound like no big deal. I didn't want her worrying about becoming a widow every time I flew somewhere. But she worried anyway.

Years earlier, during my four tours in Vietnam with the Army, there were likewise several occasions when extraordinary lifesaving events happened to me, but nothing quite as dramatic or unequivocal as "the extremely near miss" in the Cessna. People ask me, "Why did you do it? Why dive?" I have no answer, other than, "I believe it was God." I never did it again, so I still don't know how long the DME would have taken to recalculate, and I'm no longer curious about it.

Eric and I had a special relationship after that, as if I were anointed.

In 1979, I flew my family to the beach at Oceano in my Cessna. Kelly is carrying Michael, and Thomas and Tim are on the left; Nathan and curly-haired Patrick are on the right. This is one of my favorite memories: we walked barefoot to the beach, played for a couple of hours, and then flew home. I wish we had done it even more.

Chapter 12
BIG TIME FOMO
Mid-June 2006

As I lay in the hospital, unable to speak or move or take care of myself in any way, I was now buoyed by the thought of God's control of my life. I loved the stories my family would tell me about what they had all done while I was in the induced coma.

The waiting room was indeed taken over by my family, with the hospital's approval. Kelly and my children were there regularly, and it was one big love festival as they waited for me to come home.

"Dad, we're all together, praying for you," Elizabeth said when she visited. "We weren't sure you would make it at first. Some days, there's bad news, and we talk and pray. And then, good news—we celebrate. I'm so relieved you're awake and doing so well!"

Over the following days, I would be visited by excellent technicians practicing all the modalities involved in healing, such as physical therapists, speech therapists, radiology technicians, breathing specialists, swallowing experts, and the usual phlebotomists and lab technicians.

Each day, around 7:00 a.m., the x-ray tech would come and slide a panel under my back, focus the portable machine on my chest, take one exposure, and pack up—gone in three minutes. Turns out they'd been doing this for at least a week, even on the RotoRest, and could accurately trace the amount of water I was removing from my lungs.

Then, around 9:00 a.m., the doctor in charge of my case would stop by to check my chart. He was accompanied by a cadre of about seven or eight interns, and as he reviewed my status with them in a loud voice, I found it edifying to get a sense of the picture they had of my condition! One of the interns, Dr. Swarna, could see I was distraught with the tubes and the helplessness. She looked into my eyes and told me, "We see that you're progressing very nicely, and it shouldn't be long before we can remove the ventilator, and you can breathe on your own. Just be patient." Her smile and the encouraging look in her eyes buoyed my spirits.

The physical therapist, who typically manned the burn unit, would come by in the late morning and make me move my arms and legs, which I found painful but necessary. The effect of being comatose for almost three weeks had serious consequences on my muscles. At this point, I had lost nearly thirty pounds, and it was practically all muscle. And my strength was gone from the muscles I had left; I longed to gain it back.

I found myself hoping that the missing pieces of my memory would return. I spent considerable time attempting to recall what happened after I took water into my lungs. It's as if I could almost grasp it, and then nothing.

But several interesting things happened over the next week, adding a unique flavor to the experience and making it even more memorable for me.

Thomas and Elizabeth bought me a new, state-of-the-art iPod, loaded with music they knew I would appreciate, on June 16th—the 17th is my birthday—delivering it as an early gift, since they knew I was somewhat locked in my world! I marveled at it, but alas, I was unable to work the simple controls and couldn't even put the headset on to listen to it because my hands weren't strong enough yet. After about three more days, I was able to use it and found it a true blessing.

The drugs I was getting made my blood pressure high, making it impossible to sleep, so I was constantly drifting in and out of a twilight state after three days. It took about that long for me to finally turn my head and look around, see the nursing station and the other patients in the ICU. There was a Hispanic guy who'd been in a serious car accident and was recovering, and this was during the soccer World Cup. One of the nurses brought in a TV for him to watch, which delighted him greatly. But the volume was not low, and the broadcast was entirely in Spanish. He slept for five hours and then was awake for one, so I had the TV removed when he was about to be moved out of the ICU.

One consequence of having a tube delivering air to the lungs is that mucus can build up in it and must be suctioned out regularly. When the buildup becomes significant, it "burbles" and feels ominous, as if it could impede the flow of air, which it would eventually. A choking and gasping episode would quickly develop. It didn't, in my case, because the staff was so good at checking on me. An easy fix for this was "suctioning" the mucus out, and it was then collected in a bag on the side of the bed. The process requires a technician to perform it, which takes approximately ten seconds. The staff developed a "thumbs-up" sign that I would give whenever someone was walking by to let them know when I needed help. They would immediately stop and do the suctioning. This worked pretty well. However, on several occasions, staff members walking by who were unfamiliar with the protocol would give a thumbs up back and say, "Looking good, man!" The nursing station would react quickly.

Eventually, over those few days, most of the waiting room came into the ICU to see me, even though I couldn't even smile, but that was also very special.

I was pretty sure being able to communicate in some fashion would make recovery and healing happen faster and lift all of our spirits because my visitors and my family were still thinking I might be brain-injured. I didn't feel like I was, but I wouldn't be certain until others I was trying to communicate with could verify it. Plus, I had a feeling that I wasn't remembering everything I should. I wanted to ask them all about what had happened when I drowned and since. What did I miss? I was getting frustrated. Turns out my kids were too!

We tried eye blinks, but they didn't work very well. So, Thomas wrote the alphabet on a big sheet of paper in six lines—Z being the sixth line. Then, with a whiteboard to log my responses, I would squeeze someone's finger to indicate which line, and squeeze again for the letter in that line. This way I could finally communicate! When we had perfected the system, the first thing I spelled was, "What's my bilirubin?" Everyone roared because it was immediately obvious I wasn't brain-dead! Frankly, I didn't know the significance of the number except that it had to do with liver function, but I figured that would impart a message—it did.

Using this method, we had several impactful "conversations" over the next week. Somehow, I remembered a movie, *The Diving Bell and the Butterfly*, which expressed the intensity of emotions one would feel being alone in a world where everything is moving and you cannot. It's a biography of a Frenchman who wakes from a three-week coma, like me, after suffering a severe cerebral vascular accident. He's diagnosed with "locked-in syndrome," where his body is paralyzed but his brain is fine, although he only has one eye that works. I must have seen a preview of this movie on a television that a nurse brought into the ICU while I was unable to sleep. It was far worse than what I was going through, but now it was easy for me to imagine what the guy was experiencing. Having this means of communication—the finger-squeezing—really made the mute experience bearable. Not tolerable, but bearable!

There was a window on my right with a shade, and by looking out of it, I could tell whether it was day or night. It would occasionally light up with a very bright light for a few seconds—I found this irregular apparition curious. I asked a nurse what the light was. I was told that Andrea Brown, CHP, would shine her spotlight on that window as a "Hey Thom!" whenever their helicopter brought in a new patient. Their job entailed responding to motor vehicle accidents throughout the county, so they regularly transported injured people. What a special treat for me to be greeted like that! She occasionally dropped into the waiting room to see how I was doing and quickly became part of the family.

Andrea was able to say some of the things she would have said back when they picked me up along the river. Thomas came in and told me what she had said to them.

"Listen, guys, when we approach an injury/recovery situation, a group of people is usually sequestered away from the body, and the body is all by itself," Andrea said. "We were surprised to see the group of rafters around the victim, your dad, who we hadn't expected to find alive, since the accident had happened so much earlier.

"I was pretty sure that was the last time you boys would see your dad alive," she said. "Although he was breathing, barely, odds were terrible that he'd survive even for a day. I've seen a lot of drownings like this, and they don't turn out well. Especially when he's not young, he has diabetes, and he went more than twenty-two minutes without oxygen!"

My family appreciated Andrea all the more for sharing that with them, and so did I.

One afternoon, Patrick and Elizabeth asked if I needed anything. I spelled out "Panis Angelicus," a song Patrick sang a cappella when he was in the Shubert Boys Choir. They promptly sang it for me.

"Yep, Dad, we enjoy singing for you," Elizabeth said. "We sing together a lot."

Made my heart glad, and if I could have smiled, I would have! Then, as an encore, Patrick sang "The River," which is a Garth Brooks song. "I will sail my vessel till the river runs dry. I'll never reach my destination if I never try. So I'll sail my vessel till the river runs dry …" It was so intense, so apropos, so moving, and sung so well that everyone stopped what they were doing to listen. The entire ICU staff even teared up. I was silently awed. Patrick loved singing in a deep voice, like Randy Travis, and sang Italian songs at Macaroni Grill for diners.

Several friends of my children delivered food and numerous homemade casseroles and desserts to the group in the waiting room, including Outback Steakhouse, Macaroni Grill, Tahoe Joe's, and a variety of pizzas. My sons had all worked at places that served dinner, something Kelly and I encouraged! Elizabeth's friend even brought in a DVR for the television Liz had bought a couple of weeks before, which helped keep the little guys entertained.

On my birthday, June 17th, the whole family took turns visiting me. There was cake, cards, gifts, and a whole lot of love. I was worn out, but appreciated this birthday more than any other.

Whole families came to the ICU to check on me and my kids. It was, after all, quite a party going on! All the cousins, uncles, aunts, friends of friends, and their children, many of whom were staying overnight in case I awoke, spent time in that waiting room. What fun! I was experiencing severe FOMO—Fear Of Missing Out! They were having a party, sharing a vast amount of love and appreciation for their family, much of it memorialized in a diary in which they wrote inscriptions, some to me and some recounting the experience of the family gathered in that waiting room. I am deeply touched when I read these, as they feel like love letters.

Note: Here's a [sic] for all of them below as they were sometimes written hurriedly and not spell checked, and are authentically unedited by me and my editor—no one ever imagined they would be in a book one day!

Some entries from that journal beginning May 29:

"A vigil is a special dynamic that includes some intense spiritual, emotional, and psychological support. This has certainly been the case as so many of your immediate and extended family have gathered at UMC and at locations all across the US and the world. The CHP EMTs came by to check on your progress and were amazed that so many people have heard about you, though it didn't make the news! The prayer chain has been linking up everywhere. We are all so hopeful with every report from the medical staff, yet they remind us that you are still critical and have a long way to go before you're whole and back to your normal ornery self. While we trust your care to a team of dedicated medical professionals, it is clear to all that your future is in the hands of God. He will determine your fate. The fervent prayers of so many have been offered on your behalf. We once again have come together for one of our own. We're not ready for you to go. I hope the Lord isn't ready for you either." –Dwight

That was written by my brother, recalling that we came together when our sister Rosemary's daughter, Joanna, was killed in a car accident. Many of the entries in the diary are written in letter form to me, like Dwight's.

"I am amazed by the great attitude shown by your boys and Liz through this experience. Tim has been THE MAN with the numbers, always ready for an update. Pat and Nate have been the PR (public relations) reps, keeping everyone up to date. Mike took care of the food and drinks. Thomas couldn't leave for the longest time, but he finally got some sleep last night. You are truly blessed. The events on Saturday were astonishing. Everyone present will never be the same. We are excited to learn what you went through, if you recall. I am excited to see you on your feet again. The moment you blinked for us on request was one of the greatest moments I have experienced. Looking at Thomas, he was relieved to be able to finally stop pumping! You've got a lot left, and I look forward to reflecting on this soon. Love ya, Jeremy" (My brother Gordie's son.)

"Mr. Miller, in the time I've gotten to know you, you've secured a place in my heart. You were always the one to make sure that everyone around felt at home, at ease. You are an inspiration to me and I can never thank you enough for that. I told Elizabeth that if ever there were a man to pull through this, it's you! You are a fighter. Your family are the best people I've had the luck to know. You show everyone what the words 'family love' mean. Always, Christian Boeving" (He's a renown bodybuilder and actor—Elizabeth's friend.)

"Elizabeth and I were just in visiting with you. You look good today. Your color has come back and your extremities are nice and warm. They are pumping a bunch of meds into you and we can't all help but think they need to just give you your regular dosage of vitamin C & E. The problem with that is they probably can't handle the gas a few hours later! Tim has been amazing throughout this process. He, like always, is a sponge, sucking up all the medical terms and facts and reiterating them to Mama Kelly and the family like a champ. He is so wonderful at reminding everyone of each positive step you are taking. Also telling us again you are living proof that miracles still happen. Stay tuned… Love, Katie" (My daughter-in-law.)

That diary of sorts made me weep when I read it. I'll never forget how it made me feel back then.

Moving forward, Kelly and I had just sold our home on Bullard Ave, west of Fresno, in a fig orchard, the month before the rafting trip, and picked out a brand-new, huge house that had been built on the vacant lot next to Tim's home on the bluff, above the San Joaquin River in northwest Fresno. We'd watched it being built and decided it was for us. Thomas was able to negotiate the purchase, and escrow was ready to open. Kelly brought the notary into the hospital with the documents, and I "signed" them. Since I was intubated and too weak to even hold a pen, they held my hand and moved it as I would have, if I could have, to create my signature.

Kelly later explained to me what was going on for her while I was stuck on the ventilator, unable to help.

"I was still trying to put this house deal together—filling out loan papers and trying to decide various things," Kelly said. "I didn't know how you were going to come out of this. Do we buy this house or not? Is it just going to be for me? Or what if you're disabled? What if you've got brain injuries that won't allow you to go upstairs? I felt like I was in limbo, but I had to set a direction. So I decided to buy it, and I'm still glad we went ahead with the deal. It turned out great, thank You, Jesus. When you signed the closing papers in the hospital, I was so relieved. Wasn't it so good of the escrow officer to come here? She was a good friend, and she got all the paperwork completed and notarized it—did the whole thing."

Moving to a new home is always such a pain, but this new house was something I couldn't wait to live in! It was very roomy, and I imagined all the things I wanted to buy and do to make it feel like ours. It gave me something to look forward to. And now, it looked like my wife would have to ramrod the "Brobdingnagian" effort of moving in without me. (In Jonathan Swift's *Gulliver's Travels*, Gulliver is shipwrecked on the Island of Brobdingnag, a land of giants. Hence, any tremendous job can be considered Brobdingnagian.)

And thus, a new chapter in the life of a former—hopefully—hoarder began.

I love this shot of family and friends in the ICU waiting room. This went on the whole time I was hospitalized. Jeb & Julie are in the top left, rafting guide Kevin, Sophie Mukwana Gitonga (an honorary member of the Miller clan), my nephew Andy, Patrick, and, seated in front, Thomas, my mother Loretta Miller, and my sister Joyce.

Michael, Patrick, CHP helicopter pilot Paul Dwyer, CHP helicopter EMT Andrea Brown, Nathan, Thomas, Greg, and Tim gathering at the hospital waiting for me to heal.

Chapter 13
PASS GO AND COLLECT $200
Monday, June 19, 2006

Finally, my PEEP score and oxygen readings were within the standard range. After a brief discussion, Dr. Javed ordered the tube removed.

"We've been advising you to practice breathing forcefully to raise your PEEP, and it looks like you're getting a handle on it," he said. "Your metrics are almost where we need them to be to remove the tubes from your throat. We can do a few more simple tests, and you'll be ready. I know you've heard that once we remove these things, we only put them back in to save lives. Currently, your metrics are satisfactory, but if an issue arises and you require intervention, it becomes very challenging. So, we want to be sure your lungs are working well enough on their own before we take them out."

I nodded, and I'm sure my eyes were big. I wanted the tubes out ASAP, provided I was far enough along in my recovery that I could make it. Dr. Volkova assured me I had recovered to parameters that predicted a positive outcome.

And Dr. Javed was ready. We then moved on to the next step.

I was placed in a chair next to the bed, sitting upright, and they turned off the ventilator to see how I would respond. In half an hour, my oxygen dropped too low, so they decided to give the vent another day. I couldn't feel the difference, so I couldn't see the failure coming. However, they watched the gauges throughout the test, which allowed them to recognize that I needed more PEEP practice. I did the deep-breathing exercises all afternoon and into the evening.

The next morning, June 20th, we repeated the test, and I passed. The doctor then gave the green light to remove the tubes, so I had a brief mental celebration. The procedure was uncomfortable, but nothing like being intubated, and the relief was instant. The feeling of having the tubes removed was like what you'd feel if you were to swallow a two-foot-long piece of very thick spaghetti and then slowly pull it back out. It almost stimulated my gag reflex, but I focused on suppressing it. Not painful but highly unusual. When they had put the tubes in, I was unconscious, so I hadn't known what to expect.

The next day, Michael shared a neat story about what his church did for me. "Right around the time you got off the ventilator, I heard that you had made a turn for the better overnight. The cool thing is, I had spoken with my pastor from First Baptist Church of Long Beach on the phone the night before and told him about your situation. He informed me that he had added us to the church's prayer log. That means everybody at church had prayed for you, Dad, and our family. Maybe fifteen to twenty minutes later, you could breathe on your own. This is epic!"

Greg was praying too. "When your breathing tube was removed yesterday, I became fully confident that there is somebody up there," he said. He pointed to the sky. "You know, watching after us. There have been many instances when God has intervened in my life and brought about what was needed. So I prayed and said, 'Hey, God, I know you may want to take my dad, and that's okay if you do, but I've got some unfinished business, and I want to spend more time with him.'

"As you know, there was a long time when I was a different person." Greg looked down at his clasped hands. "I was young, naive, and a dumbass, frankly. Then, just as I began to develop a more mature relationship with you and got to know you as an adult, this happened. So, I didn't want God to take you now."

My heart was filled with joy at what my boys were experiencing.

I visited with family and friends, and being able to talk again was wonderful. My voice was almost normal, but not all parts of my mouth were in sync. After being immobilized for three weeks, the muscles all over my body had atrophied. Nowhere was it more evident than on my tongue. My speech was slurred, and I was choking on the little bit of water I could now drink with a straw. I had never considered what it would be like if the epiglottis—the small, muscular patch of tissue which acts as a trap door for the bronchial tube from the throat to the lungs—were not working correctly. Still, since it had tubes pressing against it for so long, it's no wonder it was having problems.

The odds of my having come out of this accident with relatively good health and cognitive skills seemed not to be in my favor, but so much of this adventure had been miraculous. It seemed, somehow, the odds had shifted!

For the next two days, I was regularly visited by the speech therapist, Courtney Young, who gave me exercises to practice. "See how I'm hugging my teeth as I start in front, like this, and move to the back, slowly, and then to the front again. First the top, then the bottom. It looks simple, but when your tongue won't do what you need it to do, you're going to have to move it slowly. The faster you can go, the sooner you'll get full use of your tongue again." I was surprised at how hard it was to move my tongue along my teeth, exploring my mouth. I had never considered my tongue to be compromised, so this was a new concept to me.

Courtney would get right in my face and show me an exercise with her tongue, which I had to repeat and practice over and over. "I'm going to be checking on you regularly, so practice these moves! I know it looks ridiculously simple, but it will take you at least a week to master these exercises. You're not going anywhere for a while, so practice whenever you think of it." Improvement was surprisingly rapid, although I continued to have a problem with some consonants that lasted another month.

Drinking fluids was a real problem. To prevent aspiration, they would only let me have fluids mixed with a thickening agent, which made the water like paste. Sometimes it was so thick I could almost chew it. Finally, I complained to Courtney, and she immediately discussed it with my nurse.

"I'm going to teach him a new trick that will fix this, but it's not a cure," Courtney said to my nurse. "He'll still need the thickener until he's no longer under hospital care."

She taught me the "chin tuck," where I would hold the fluid in my mouth, tilt my head toward my chest, lead with my chin, and then swallow. This effectively closed the epiglottis, allowing swallowing to work without choking. Very clever.

Another thing I experienced was the loss of my sense of smell and taste. Gone. I wasn't bothered by that because I knew it was the result of the drugs I'd been given, and I expected to recover from it eventually. I'd been told to expect temporary effects, and it wasn't hurting me

---

Because I was no longer requiring constant attention, they moved me out of the ICU on June 22 and into "step down," a "transition" room, with one other bed. ICU beds, after all, are minimal and used only in the worst-case scenarios. I was glad to be well enough to move out! I was there for probably an hour when another patient was brought in, and he was in extreme pain. He had been an engineer on a freight train that had just passed through Madera going south, toward Fresno. Somehow, the track signals had malfunctioned, and another freight, northbound, had passed the side rail and was headed straight at him at fifty-five miles per hour. He had no time to slow down.

"How come you couldn't just jump out?" I asked.

"When you're going faster than forty, your odds of surviving a jump are terrible. I knew that, so I just braced for impact as best I could. I sat down with my back against the front and prayed. I think it could have been worse."

The devastating impact was huge, derailing both locomotives, and he was extracted by the medical crew very carefully. Besides several broken ribs and some fractured vertebrae, the impact had split his pelvis in half. At the hospital, they were able to deal with everything but the pelvis and had to wait until he had stabilized from the trauma before they could operate. The pain was constant and intense, and he had a terrible time just lying on his side. My issues felt like nothing compared to his, and I was overwhelmed with empathy.

After about four hours, they moved him out, I guess to operate on his pelvis, finally, and put him back together.

That afternoon, another guy was brought in, this one from a motorcycle accident. The CHP was present with him to gather a report on what happened. I could hear their entire conversation.

The CHP officer asked him what happened.

His injuries consisted of abrasions on the entire left side of his body, from his face to his ankle, embedded with sand. It was ground into his skin, making his whole torso look like permanent sandpaper. Ouch. Although the medical staff had cleansed it, the sand was not coming off easily.

"This road rash all over the side of my body hurts like hell, officer, but they gave me some medication, and the pain has subsided a bit. I can answer your questions."

"Okay. How'd this happen?"

"I was cruising along in the fast lane when some guy in the lane next to me swerved into my lane and cut me off. I guess he didn't see me. Happens a lot to bikers. When I went down in the sand, I skidded on my stomach for a long way but didn't hit anything, thank God."

"How fast were you going, and what kind of vehicle was it that cut you off?"

"It happened so fast that I didn't notice what kind of car it was—it could have been a Chevy. I was probably doing about fifty-five." The injured man winced from pain.

The CHP said that the guy's bike's front forks were broken, but he might be able to save the rest of the bike. "We're going to write this up as a 'hit and run' even though you weren't hit by another vehicle, and you can get a copy of the report for the insurance company from our district office."

The two officers politely wished him well and left. About an hour later, two of his motorcycle buddies came to visit him.

"Damn, you look like hell," one of his buddies said. "But I gotta say, I imagined you'd be all wrapped up in Plaster of Paris or something, with all kinds of broken bones. You're one lucky hosehead! What happened?"

"I just finished putting those extended forks on and was trying it out. I was doing about seventy in the fast lane when they started to wobble, and before I could slow down, they came apart. Sure glad I was in the fast lane next to the sand because that asphalt would have wiped me out. That sand looks bad now, but it was a blessing!"

They left, promising to meet him at his shop in a few weeks.

I just scratched my head at what I'd heard.

I still hadn't slept for at least four days, almost exclusively because they were keeping my blood pressure higher than usual. When your blood pressure is abnormally high, as mine was, you cannot sleep. It could have had something to do with the meds I was getting, but I couldn't tell. You can rest and reflect, but you cannot fall into a deep sleep. The exhaustion was starting to get uncomfortable, but the activity around me did seem to be contributing to my inability to sleep. One of my nurses got permission to move me to a room with four beds, three of which were occupied by unconscious patients. At about 11:00 p.m., they moved me into that room. The lighting was subdued, and it was silent except for the sound of a C-PAP on one of the patients. I took two of the pills they'd given me for sleep and relaxed into a solemn rest.

About twenty minutes later, I was jolted awake as all hell broke loose. Flashing lights, the PA system announcing a "Code Blue," and the crash cart with cardiac equipment were rushed into my room with three nurses and two doctors, and more on the way. One of the semiconscious patients had experienced a heart attack, and his monitors had gone off. I watched as the crash cart team frantically worked on him. I prayed they'd faithfully do everything they could to bring him back. They finally wheeled him out on a gurney with a sheet covering him. I had no idea who he was or who his family was because I had only been a silent witness to his passing. I felt a little sadness at the fact that his last moments on earth were observed in relative loneliness. What a way to check out.

After about two hours, things finally got quiet, and I lapsed into a deep sleep. I didn't wake up until they came to move me into another room on the morning of June 23rd.

My new room had two beds, and the other bed was unoccupied. I relaxed in this new environment when the nurse brought in a visitor, Stacey Serra. She and her sister were expert guides for KRE and were fun to be around. She was the guide on the lead raft ahead of ours and part of the group responsible for bringing me ashore. She got me a Sudoku book to keep my brain busy, and we talked. She cried when she related how traumatic my event had been for her and all at KRE.

"I'm hanging up my oar," Stacey said. "Talia and I are going back to our family in Portugal. Rafting people on the Kings was fun, very fun, until your accident. Now I can't see the fun side of it anymore—only how dangerous it can be and how quickly it can change in an instant. It's just too heavy."

I tried to comfort her. "Stacey, you were there. You saw my hand grab the rope when it was across my chest, and you saw them pry my hand from the rope when they started the CPR. No way could any geezer like me hold onto the rope while being pulled in, underwater, against the snowmelt current of the Kings! You *know* God was there! You were part of that! I know you were as awestruck as Thomas and Kevin were when I came back, but it unfolded on your watch. Tell me all this doesn't blow you away, and that God has allowed me to 'pass go and collect two hundred dollars!' Good came of this. Of all who were there, I am the most amazed, impressed, and thankful for you! You are a huge part of my life now!"

She smiled through tears. "I agree, and I love you too. God has his hand on you, Thom, and I will never forget feeling so close to Him, thanks to you."

Stacey and I cried together, and I explained that I felt God was using me as an example of the reality that He's always there, and she can be okay with whatever happens because He's in charge. I didn't want her to quit because of me.

"KRE needs great people, and you're one of them. Remember, in the thirty-three years KRE has existed, I'm the only casualty! And I'm alive again, thanks in part to you!"

We dried our tears, hugged for a moment, and she was gone.

Someone had asked me a day or two earlier if I thought KRE was responsible for what happened to me. I don't believe they were, but I wondered what my son Tim thought about it because he was both a nurse and an attorney, managing litigation for various hospitals, including their professional, employment, and general liability cases, which essentially involve lawsuits. The following is what Tim said, and I agreed with him.

"I don't think KRE did anything wrong. It's an act of God that it's hot on day one and then extremely cold the next. They got on the river the first day, and it was hot, so the flow was high—the water had already come down the hill from the melting snow. And the next day, it was so cold that the snow melting uphill slowed, and the water flow was reduced." Tim paused for a moment and looked out the window. He turned back to me and said, "Nobody can predict that. They go by what's happening right in front of them, factoring in what is typical. And I'm sure that that change shocked everyone who got on the river that day, from the splash and play that it was the day before to this massive Class 4, live rapid experience."

The next day, June 24th, I talked with Dr. Volkova about going home. She was the physician in charge of my case once I was no longer in the ICU.

"Your lungs are not healed yet. You might think you're okay, but you're right on the edge. You need to stay here on oxygen for another two weeks, at least, and let us bring you over the finish line." Dr Volkova was firm. I could tell she was going to throw serious cold water on me, but I'd been in serious cold water before!

"I grant you that the facilities here have just about anything a patient would need to recover, but I miss my family," I told her. "I know they've been in the waiting room, but being with them is different! Besides, my wife's meals are amazing. And you know that statistics show that injuries heal faster and better when the patient is in a loving, comfortable home setting."

"If you were to leave now, and something were to happen that required immediate intervention, you'd be all alone," Dr. Volkova reasoned. "And if you find you're having trouble breathing, we can help you here. You won't be able to get oxygen at home. The laws governing the distribution of oxygen equipment and its prescriptions are complex, and you may not have access to the oxygen you need there. That could be the difference between being alive and not."

I was not going to let her paint me into a corner with worst-case scenarios. I was healing, a situation which was beyond imagining a week ago, and I wanted the healing to continue in an environment in which I would be comfortable. "If we were to graph my progress based on the water in my lungs as demonstrated in the X-rays, I believe it would show a steady change as it diminished. What intervention could affect that, besides inhaling water again?"

Dr. Volkova agreed that I had come a long way and that my improvement was steady; short of drowning again, it was likely to continue. "But ARDS is a troublesome condition that rarely results in complete recovery. Granted, your improvement is pretty remarkable, and we weren't expecting you to be at this point by now, so you have a good argument."

"Thank you! I want to be discharged to go home as soon as my condition allows it."

"I will discuss it with the staff and we'll move toward that as soon as they concur," she said.

The next morning, June 25th, my nurse told me that I would be going home as soon as my arterial oxygen level was ninety or more. The lab tech came to get some blood. Arterial blood is taken from an artery deep in the wrist, and stabbing it with a needle was pretty painful! And it's not a little needle. She finally got it after I squirmed and complained. Two hours later, she returned to collect more, stating that the sample was inconclusive. I argued, but to no avail.

"You know, I've been in here for several weeks and had all kinds of procedures done on me, and this arterial blood draw is the most painful of them! Are you sure we've gotta do this again?"

She did it on the other wrist, over my protestations, and took it back to the lab. I lived through it, but I didn't understand why they wouldn't use the pulse oximeter number they'd been relying on. The reality is that the pulse oximeter uses "fuzzy logic" to calculate oxygen levels, much like sphygmomanometers used to measure blood pressure, and it's relatively accurate. However, a physical measurement by a human is considered more reliable, the gold standard. I understood that my recovery was a little unusual, and they just wanted to cover all the bases by ensuring all their metrics were accurate.

My arterial oxygen level was exactly ninety-two, so I was delighted when they told me I would be leaving first thing in the morning. My new home wasn't ready yet, and Kelly was working her usual ten hours a day again, so my family was going to have to surprise me somehow!

Chapter 14
NO PLACE LIKE HOME
Monday, June 26, 2006

The nurse came to get me ready to leave.

"Do you realize how incredible it is that you are well enough to leave and go home?" she said. "We have been planning on having you here for at least two more weeks, so I hate to see you go. I hope your O2 levels stay high enough, or we'll see you back here!"

"I appreciate all you folks have done for me, and if it weren't for the great care I've received, I'm sure I'd be staying longer. But like Dorothy said, 'There's no place like home.' And I need to be close to my family to recover. Thanks for being here for me."

My clothes had been brought in by the boys when they came down from the Kings River, and they were neatly packed in a bag. I was able to stand up, barely, and get fully dressed. They rolled a wheelchair in, and I got on, not realizing that my son, Thomas, was waiting outside my room.

He pushed me slowly down the hall. As we went, everyone backed up to the wall to let us pass. They all smiled at me, and a few even waved goodbye. The whole experience made me feel like I was starting a new life, and I became so happy. Thomas's car was parked at the entrance to the ER, so we were able to jump in easily. He rolled the wheelchair back in, and we were off.

"Where are we headed?" I asked.

"Nathan has a room set up for you with a king mattress on the floor so that you can drop onto it easily. Plenty of pillows in case you need to be propped up." I smiled because I could see that my family had thought of everything.

"Yes, we're going straight to Nathan's house," Kelly said. "We'll stay there and wait for the escrow on our new house to close, which is supposed to be today. It's likely to be a few days before we can move in. If the house closes escrow today, and the boys can move our stuff from storage to the new place tomorrow and Wednesday, we can move in on Thursday or Friday, the 29th or 30th. We'll still make it in June!"

As always, Kelly had everything under control.

So, where was my wife all this time? Our business, which the two of us ran from our main store in Fresno, was a retail store specializing in medical uniforms. When my father-in-law purchased it in 1995, it had four stores: Sacramento, Santa Barbara, Fresno, and Dublin. But running a three-store enterprise, with the inventory upgrades, bookkeeping, sales, and reporting to government agencies, really took both of us. We had divided the different management functions into specific areas of expertise that suited us, and we had perfected a system that worked very well. Without me, it was simply lopsided and very difficult for Kelly because she didn't know how to do many of the things I had been doing. She was already working overtime, but several modifications had made it workable for now.

We had several discussions about it together and with our children. She shared the following with them one night:

"When you're married, you have a clear delineation of your jobs and his jobs, and you don't know his jobs, and he doesn't know your jobs," she explained. "You both do them accordingly. And so, in our case, the problem was not only in our home and family environment, but also in our business. I didn't know how to do his job at the company, and he didn't know how to do mine.

"But I feel like we're all on a path. Whatever happens is the path that God put us on, and these are the things that we have to experience. So, I never questioned why this was happening to me. This was just part of the path." Kelly stopped and slowly shook her head. "But not knowing how your dad would come out of it, whether he would be mentally challenged, I felt compelled to try to keep the business going, which meant I needed to know what he did. How does he do payroll? I had no opportunity to learn that."

Kelly thought back to one evening when I was still in this hospital, and told the kids, "I was having a tough day and was exhausted after visiting with Dad. But it was sweet because I remember I went to the store after I left his bedside. It was about 6:15 p.m. and the store was closed. I was sitting in the back crying and thinking, 'What am I going to do?' She looked over at Tim and smiled.

"Tim and his wife suddenly showed up. They came in and asked, 'How can we help?'" Tim was aware of some of the tasks that needed to be done. He had worked for us at one point. "And that was one of the sweetest things that happened. All of you kids have been great, but it was especially sweet that they would go out of their way to visit the store. No call. No, they just walked through that door, ready to help."

When we got to Nathan's, I was surprised to find Elizabeth waiting for me! She had volunteered to be my constant companion for the next two weeks as my rehabilitation progressed, making sure I got everything I needed. I slept fitfully at first because I had to be elevated on pillows and slept on my side, which I'm not accustomed to. Whenever I awoke, she was sitting on the corner of the bed, silently watching me, ready to get me anything I needed, and even help me into the bathroom. I could see that Elizabeth played a crucial role in my recovery in ways I would never fully understand.

When I finally got into the shower, two things surprised me. First, I'd lost almost forty pounds, but it was all muscle. Despite not having solid food for three weeks, my paunch had not diminished. Fixing this was going to take some work! The second thing was that when I washed my hair, a substantial amount went down the drain. At first, I thought nothing of it, but after a week, the hair loss hadn't subsided, and I began to wonder if I would lose all of it. *So be it—that's what you get for poking fun at Thomas!* I started collecting it in a coffee can, calculating how much was coming off, but after a week, I stopped. Back to Alfred E Newman: "What, me worry?" Maybe it was a psychosomatic problem anyway, and there wasn't anything I knew to do to stop it.

The few days at Nathan's were great just for relaxing. The pharmaceutical regimen I had been through for three weeks had wrought havoc with my alimentary system, causing mild to severe diarrhea and some inflammation of the urethra. Consequently, I spent a considerable amount of time on the toilet, staggering back and forth to the bathroom. Later, when I got home to my new house, the first thing I did was replace the toilet seat with a cushioned seat, something I'd always scoffed at. But what a difference. When you've lost as much weight as I have, your padding is reduced all over, making extended time on the john very uncomfortable. And I was there a lot!

On Friday, June 30th, I was ready to move into my new house, and I bid goodbye to Nathan and Theresa's house—they had been a massive part of a significant step in my journey to recovery. What a treat it was for me to experience their hospitality, love, and care when I was at my most helpless.

Elizabeth began caring for me at the new house, primarily when Kelly was working. She recognized that I couldn't sleep on my back and remembered that one of her neighbors in West Los Angeles had a hospital bed she wanted to get rid of. Elizabeth acquired it and then had it transported to Fresno. It was heavy, but my boys picked it up, brought it upstairs—we had circular stairs, so that wasn't easy—and set it up in my new bedroom—another Brobdingnagian task. I was so very proud of them.

The immediate relief I experienced when sleeping on the raised mattress was astonishing. I'm sure that bed was another significant factor in my progressive recovery. Kelly concurred.

My mother visited not long after we moved in, and Kelly told her, "Elizabeth spends lots of time with her dad." Kelly patted Elizabeth's hand. "She's a good caregiver. It's awesome. She knows I have to go to work. She knows she can't go to work for me, so the best thing she can do is stay here. And I do have someone that I can leave the store with, so I am coming and going all the time."

"Now that Dad is home, I want to stay with him," Elizabeth said. "I've been living with my cousin, Chrissy, in L.A., so it isn't too hard for me to come home and stay with Dad. I spend all day with him, doing whatever he needs. That's me, though. I'm going to be here for the people I love.

"I admit, I'm doing things for Dad that no daughter would want to do, though, like helping him shower because he can't stand alone, or holding him tightly as we walk a bit because he can't move without assistance. Getting him to the bathroom is not super glamorous. But I love being with him. It's a super special time for us together. By the way, he has always been athletic. I think he's probably doing as much as he can to recover. Totally. He works very hard at it. He got a sauna, and that is helping. He keeps trying to remove those toxins and clear everything out of his system."

My mother beamed with pride at her granddaughter.

Time was passing quickly. On Monday, July 10th, Kelly took me to the VA hospital in Fresno to check my status in their system. Because I had previously applied for treatment for my diabetes and was approved for "service-connected" disability, I qualified for treatment at any VA hospital. The PT (physical therapy) treatments prescribed at UMC, along with other considerations, needed to be set up, and the VA has a tremendous PT department.

I was assigned a primary doctor and made an appointment for a week later, but when I arrived, he had me sit in the waiting room for nearly an hour before seeing me. I experienced excruciating pain sitting in the hard chair and was quickly exhausted, but he didn't seem to understand my issues and was not empathetic at all. I felt he was treating me as if he considered me a malingerer, and I immediately sought a replacement doctor.

The VA gave me options, and I chose Sharrod Behnam, one of the interns who had been watching my progress at UMC. We met in his office at the VA hospital and had immediate camaraderie.

"I think we'll be fine because I know what you've been through, and I think I know what I can do to help your recovery. I'm very proud to be part of your recovery team."

He stepped out momentarily and returned with Dr Swarna because he knew I held her in high regard. I was overjoyed to see her—

she had given me such hope when I was intubated that I felt an almost spiritual bond with her.

"Of all the doctors at UMC who were caring for me and watching my progress, you are the one doctor I connected with most, whether you knew it or not. You were a lifeline for me because I could see hope and love in your eyes. I felt that I wouldn't depart if you were there for me. I know that sounds a bit sappy, but that's how I felt. All the communication I had with anyone was through eye contact, and yours was comforting." I hugged her, which made for an embarrassing moment, but, oh well!

One thing was sure: my spiritual life was growing to a degree that I had never experienced. I deeply and thoroughly believed that God sent his Son, Jesus, to die for me and for all of us. One day, sitting in my beautiful home, feeling very blessed, I thought back to an experience in Vietnam, when I had begun to get only the tiniest glimpse of what that sacrifice meant. But now, after my own death experience, I comprehended it in a very personal way.

Chapter 15
FLASHBACK: HE TOOK MY PLACE
December 1967

I joined the US Army in January 1966 and, after four months of training, was sent to Vietnam. The Boeing 707 carried about one hundred thirty of us to Tan Son Nhut airbase in Saigon. We deplaned, grabbed our duffel bags, and eight of us fell out of formation to be bused to our unit, MACV (Military Assistance Command, Vietnam). The others went on to Long Binh Junction.

We were driven to the Koelper Compound, a five-story hotel with a restaurant on the ground floor. It was surrounded by barbed wire and guarded by fortified sandbagged posts and heavily armed guards. All MACV personnel entering or leaving the country were processed through Koelper.

I found out that I would stay at Koelper for three days, "acclimating" and relaxing in my decent digs while being served three meals a day. During the day, we attended various sessions designed to introduce us to Vietnam, its customs, culture, and more. I struck up a friendship with the cook. He told me that "Koelper" was named for Donald E. Koelper, a captain who lost his life saving scores of lives during a VC terrorist bombing.

By "VC," he meant Viet Cong, using the phonetic alphabet "Victor Charlie." Sometimes, it was reduced to "Charlie" or "Charles." They were the Vietnamese Communists, a military branch of the National Liberation Front (NLF), and were under the command of the Central Office for South Vietnam.

At the end of three days, at zero-six-thirty, I boarded a C-130 transport. After we were high enough to clear all the mountains, we circled toward the ocean and Qui Nhon, a harbor city and fishing community. We dropped in at the airstrip easily and taxied to the end of the runway, where they waited for me to disembark.

They were gone in five seconds, heading up to Da Nang. They left me all alone at the end of the airstrip, where a parachute canopy was strung between three palm trees.

I then noticed that someone had strapped a field phone to one of the palm trees, and next to it was a sign that read, "MACV ring 2x," so I did. I was able to get someone to give me a ride to our compound.

The Jeep driver who picked me up was a quiet PFC (Private First Class) who drove me to the MACV Compound. "How many guys are there in Team 22?" I asked.

"We have about thirty guys who work at BaGi, the Division HQ, and another twenty guys attached as security guards. Each officer has their own section. The compound used to be a French villa on the beach, so you get a nice breeze every night—it's nice."

Here we go again, special treatment. How do I deserve this?

I was excited to be getting where I was supposed to be, finally!

I had been trained as a clerk typist, which meant I would be in the typing pool at the G-1 Administration section of Team 22.

"Miller, we don't need any more clerks," Lt. Hinton said. He ran the G-1 (Administration) section. "I'm going to send you down to G-3—maybe they could use you." He pointed to another building fifty yards away, and I set out for the short walk to G-3, which was the Operations section. The reassignment was highly fortuitous for me. There, I would work with one captain, two lieutenants, and a senior sergeant. The latter was Sgt. Bizek. He told me I would eventually be promoted to E-6.

It looked like I had a meaningful job.

"Welcome to G-3, Miller," Sergeant Bizek said. "We're glad to have you aboard. Can you type?"

"Sergeant Bizek, I can type! Try me!" I liked the idea.

He had been having to type the daily situation report, and he hated it. Sgt Bizek was, needless to say, happy to have me delegate this to him. It became enjoyable after a while, thanks to some modifications I made.

I quickly became busy, maintaining our maps with current troop positions and the status of any operations we were assisting with. I also operated our SB-22 switchboard, interfacing with the rest of the world on behalf of Team 22. If you were to call our Team from Saigon, Pleiku (pronounced "play-coo"), or anywhere else, I would answer and connect you with the office or officer you were seeking. It was special and even sort of fun.

"This is Specialist Johnson in Pleiku. Who the hell are you?" That was the first call I got when I started. After Johnson got to know me, we became fast friends and shared many enjoyable experiences. He was the switchboard operator at the II Corps MACV Headquarters in Pleiku and had held that position for six months. He was loaded with information, which would make my life a lot easier.

Once, while discussing something with Johnson in Pleiku, I heard an increase in static, and a Vietnamese-sounding voice came on and said, "Say again."

It was Charles!

Team 22 had a helicopter waiting on our helipad every day, at the ready for whatever our Senior Advisor, Lt. Colonel Cameron, wanted to do. Sometimes, he'd make a quick flight to one of the ARVN (Army of the Republic of Vietnam) battalions with his counterpart, Colonel Ly, Commander of the 22nd ARVN Division, or they'd watch the troops attacking an NVA (North Vietnamese Army) position. They called that a "command and control" flight. Lt. Colonel Cameron would check in with the G-3 Air—right next to my office—and tell us what his plans were. Otherwise, the chopper would sit there until around 3:00 p.m., when it would return to the aviation battalion it came from.

At the end of every month, our chopper would visit all the units we had in the field—a day-long trip—delivering mail and payroll to about thirty locations. The MACV Team was interspersed throughout the DTA (Division Tactical Area) under the 22nd Division's control, which covered a large area. Because I was "the map guy from G-3," I could go on this trip anytime and often did. One of my responsibilities was to maintain the radio in G-3 all night during operations, so I spoke regularly with all our advisors. Some of them were friends. Rarely did they encounter enemy fire on this helicopter trip, and we had never had any casualties. One lieutenant, two sergeants, and I would usually go.

During the fourth quarter of 1967, I had been in G-3 for two tours. I had extended my tour six months—eventually three times—so that my brother Jim, a Green Beret medic, couldn't come to Vietnam. He was eager to be sent, as he was part of a team that had come over together without him. However, the Army wouldn't allow two brothers to serve in the same war zone. I knew Green Beret medics had a short lifespan, being targeted explicitly by VC—I'd heard this from the 6th Special Forces liaison officer, whom I'd see in G-3 once a month.

Our advisory team had all moved out of Qui Nhon to the billets at Ba Gi, to save us from the semi-dangerous daily drive and into some hastily assembled "hooches"—six functional stick buildings with rooms for four single bunks each. Two of the bunks in mine were occupied by PFC Hanson and PFC Roberts—both were assigned to G-2, Intelligence, and were very quiet. They did not converse with anyone. It seemed like the G-2 men were all like that, very secretive about everything.

It was at this time that SP4 Dave French arrived at BaGi and became my third roommate. He was assigned to G-1, Administration, as a typist. He was a great guy, and we got along well.

I had seen Dave at G-1, but our paths never crossed. He had seemed like a nice guy, with a pleasant personality. I don't remember who approached whom, but we became friends, and being roommates made our friendship even stronger. He was about six-one, while I was six-three, and we were among the tallest guys on the team. Whenever we had to be in formation, which only happened once or twice, we were arranged by height. Dave would be next to me.

To stay in touch with reality, he purchased a record player and assembled a small record collection. He'd turn on some soft music in the evenings before we turned the light out. Dave's favorite band was

The Association, and he played their song "Windy" regularly on his record player, which was okay with me. It soon became one of my favorites. The lyrics contained a lot of symbolism that I eventually came to appreciate. "And Windy has wings to fly above the clouds…" Great lyrics! It was the kind of music that, once you've heard it, sticks with you all day. He played it a lot, and since I was the senior EM (enlisted man) in the room (I was an E-5 at that point), the two G-2 guys said nothing!

But we were bored. We wanted to do something else when we had time off. The Viet Cong usually didn't bother us, probably because we were supporting their underground economy. But once in a while, they'd come in and open fire on any US troops in certain bars, so we were eager to find an after-hours alternative to downtown drinking.

Booze is the bane of military guys, simply because it eases the starkness between being in the prime of life and being forced into an unnatural loneliness, living without the comfort of a partner to share life with, and facing unknown mortal dangers every day. We all tended to gravitate to the pub at the end of the day, where we could develop friendships. In the early days of my life with MACV, we'd go to the usually sleezy bars in downtown Qui Nhon and drink a Vietnamese beer, "bah me bah"—the Vietnamese words for "thirty-three," which we swore had added alcohol, like maybe formaldehyde, that caused severe headaches. We drank it anyway.

One night, I asked Sergeant Bizek, "Since we don't have a curfew like the men in the US units, don't you think it's pretty scary for us to be going into town to bars in the evenings? The MPs sweep the bars for troops out past curfew, and suddenly, we MACV types are all alone."

"Of course it is, so don't get caught down there sucking your thumb. Exercise caution, and you'll survive. Charles is always looking for victims, and lonely Gis (enlisted men) are first on the list. So when the MPs come around, you'd be smart to get back to the compound. However, the Senior Advisor has approved a project that the

G-4 guys are working on—namely, an EM Club for us Enlisted Men. So changes are coming."

Dave and I looked at each other, trying not to burst out laughing from the sheer joy of knowing we'd soon have a place to go and enjoy ourselves that was specifically for us.

Our EM Club opened in the summer of 1967, giving us something to do when we were off duty. We could hang out at the bar! Dave and I would often go there after work.

One night, I noticed that Dave was drinking scotch at the Club. "Dave, I see you like scotch! How'd you get into that?"

"When I was in clerk training, we had a sergeant who played cards—a big guy who was a nice fellow. I learned a lot from him. Anyway, he'd go through a whole bottle of scotch in an evening playing Texas hold-em. He did not take well to conflict! If he ran out, he'd tell me, 'French, I'm gettin' a case of the black-ass here. I need a refill.' I'd hustle up another bottle of Johnnie Walker, and things would cool down. I tried his Red Label and got used to it because I had to have a spare for him. I discovered that it's pretty good stuff."

"Red Label, eh? What's the difference between that and Black Label?"

"Try it. Black is a lot smoother. It's nice, but it's expensive. Red works just fine."

"Good grief, you're right! I can tell the difference!"

Dave and I would often spend an hour or two just talking about the Army, and we pretty much agreed on most of our feelings about being in Vietnam.

One morning, at the end of December, a pay run was due. This was when someone would pick up everyone's paychecks by helicopter and return to distribute them. Even though there was no place to spend a paycheck or even cash it, the Army would still issue pay every month in "military payment certificates," or MPCs—like Monopoly money. Soldiers could spend it at the PX (Post Exchange), which was like a big Target, or use it to play poker. Later, if you were leaving the country, you could convert it into greenbacks.

I was assigned to go on this run to our field units, and I began gathering my field gear—canteen, rifle, three magazines of ammo, and helmet—to take with me. Just then, Dave French approached me and begged me to let him take the run. "You get to go all over the place, see stuff, fly around. Come on, please? Let me go!"

"Dave, it makes for a long day. Are you ready for that? They don't give you ear protection, so all day hearing 'whop-whop' is going to give you a headache! Besides, when I'm on all-night duty in G-3, I talk to all these guys on the radio. I know them. And, yeah, you'd love them if you met them, but they don't know you."

"Aww, come on, Thom. You know how boring my life is around here. Give me a break! I would be forever grateful if you would let me take your place, just this once. G-1 doesn't need me today, so the timing is perfect. Please! And, oh, hell yes, I can handle the helicopter noise. I can handle it!" He got to me.

Lt. Jennings was scheduled to be the paymaster on this trip, so he had to approve the switch.

"Lieutenant Jennings, Dave French would like to replace me on this flight. Would that be okay? G-1 doesn't need him for the day."

"No prob," Lt. Jennings said. "But he'd better not get whiny on me."

I told Dave he had the green light. He was so excited that he was breathless when he went down to the helipad.

"Hey, be sure to put a magazine in that funky M-2 carbine, and give Charles a full clip if you see him. Keep that thing on full auto so you won't miss him!" I yelled at him as he boarded the Huey. He laughed and waved as he buckled in.

The next morning, I was awakened at 5:00 a.m. by Sergeant Bizek, standing by my bed. I sat up and felt instantly sick when I noticed that Dave wasn't in his bunk.

"Our chopper went down last night," Sgt. Bizek said calmly. "We think there are no survivors, so I'm taking you with me to recon the site. The ARVN Regional Forces have secured it, and they don't think enemy action caused it. I have a chopper on the pad waiting." Not trusting my voice, I just nodded.

I had to shake off the dread I felt in my stomach as reality started to set in. SFC Bizek was a no-nonsense, Camel-smoking Sergeant First Class Army warrior, not happy with a desk job in G-3, so he was always looking for excitement. This recon wasn't on his list of adventures, but it was definitely within his skill set. I was honored to be asked to accompany him, but I dreaded it.

The two of us and Captain Murkison from our G-3 flew about a half hour to a clearing on a mountainside that was secure. Our ARVN counterparts didn't like losing advisors, so they were pretty good at ensuring the places we went were safe.

"This jungle is pretty dense, but our guys have whacked a trail that should be easy to follow," Sgt. Bizek said. "We'll let them lead us to the site. In case Charles is watching us, keep your rifle ready." We hiked through the jungle for about an hour.

The crash site was located in a small clearing, approximately fifty feet below the summit of a steep mountain. When we arrived, the intense and nauseating smell of burned flesh mixed with jet fuel permeated the area. The chopper had crashed into the hillside, and it was easy to guess what had happened. After a long day of cruising our whole DTA, the pilot most likely wasn't watching his altitude in the dark. He was expecting to be out of the highlands in ten minutes and over the flat plain of the rice paddies. Or he could have nodded off for a second.

All that was left was the rotor shaft stuck vertically in the ground, with the rotor still attached. All the metal from the aircraft, even the engine, was gone. There were mounds of ash around the rotor shaft. The explosion had blown the pilot and copilot about twenty feet down the hill, still strapped in their seats.

"Sarge, these two pilots appear to have died with their eyes wide open, like maybe they were dead before the explosion blew their seats loose," Capt. Murkinson said. "Instantaneous. What do you think?

I'm not into accident reconstruction, but this is pretty open and shut, and is probably the most gruesome scene I've ever seen."

"Yeah, and that's where the smell of burned flesh is coming from—not the passengers, who are disintegrated, but the pilot there," Sgt. Bizek said, pointing at him. "Notice how the bottom of the left seat has been disintegrated entirely, including the lower part of his torso? He's still holding the helicopter's collective lever, so he was dead before his seat blew away. This was extremely sudden."

"Why don't we recon the other side of the site and see if we find anything?" I asked, thinking that the impact might have ejected others. We searched the entire site, but it was clear that all the passengers had been secured in their seats. There were no survivors, and absolutely nothing identifiable in the mound of ash; everything was completely incinerated. It was like what you'd expect to see in a crematorium. What a tragedy, since this was one of the few remaining peaks they had to clear on the way to BaGi and home.

Capt. Murkison was quietly taking notes and didn't say anything. He had been friends with Lt. Jennings and was as distressed as we were. There was no point in talking about it, so we all became introspective.

We were all somber as we silently hiked back to our chopper and flew back to BaGi. "Thom, you gather up French's stuff and get it ready to ship back to his mother in Canton, Ohio." Sgt. Bizek patted me on the back in the best display of empathy he could muster.

I gathered all of Dave's things, taking my time as I fought back tears. Placing it all neatly in a supplies box I found shoved under my bunk, I wrote a short letter to Mrs. French.

"Mrs. French, I don't know if Dave told you about me, but I have been sharing a room with him for the last four months. He was probably my best friend in our little, close-knit unit. I was very impressed by his honesty and good humor, and am proud to have known him. Yesterday, he took a long helicopter ride to visit all our field units, and he was extremely excited upon his departure. I'm sure it was probably the best ride of his life, and I was happy for him, since he had been cooped up in the Admin office since he got here. When we got word that his helicopter had crashed, I went to the scene, hoping to find some trace of him. There was nothing left but ashes. I can assure you that he died instantly and didn't suffer. I am grieved and will miss him. I know he knew Jesus, and I am sure we will see him again someday. May the peace of the Lord be with you. Specialist Thom Miller."

I let myself weep for a couple of minutes, and then took the box to the outgoing mail receptacle in the G-1 office. And life went on. I grieved for a time, but in a war zone, you have to keep moving and not dwell on the daily disasters you encounter, or you'll develop issues yourself. Still, it was hard to accept, especially going to the Club without my friend.

I should have been on that flight. It was only at the last minute, literally the last minute, that Dave French took my place.

That was the only time we had a helicopter crash with fatalities in the entire time I was in Vietnam. I did not go on another pay run after that.

Every year, the Central Valley Veterans in Fresno hold a fundraising dinner called The Star-Spangled Ball. As a member of the board of directors a few years ago, I was asked to read the short tribute and explanation about the Missing Man Table, set up next to the podium. It's a table set for one, with symbolic emptiness in deference to our missing brothers. The wine glass is turned upside down, showing that he cannot toast as we can. The table is round to symbolize the unending concern we have. The napkin is open on the plate, ready for him to take his seat.

While reading the presentation that year, I paused. I had the feeling someone was watching me, not from our audience, but someone else. I looked at the table, which was, of course, empty, and suddenly, I could see Dave sitting there, smiling at me.

Oh, Dave, Dave, brother, I miss you! I had the privilege of having seven exceptional children, all because you took my place on that flight! I grieve, but I'm grateful.

I was awestruck by how real the apparition seemed. I had intentionally not thought a lot about him since 1967, when we lost him, and I was stunned to see his face. After choking back my emotions, I finished reading the presentation and regained my composure.

I was blessed to be a guest of Central Valley Honor Flight #25 in April 2023. It's an event where a whole plane load of veterans is treated to a four-day tour of Washington, D.C., including the Capitol and Arlington National Cemetery. It was truly the adventure of a lifetime, as we visited "the Wall" at the Vietnam Veterans Memorial in Washington, D.C. I found Dave's name on it and placed a piece of paper over it, etching the name with a pencil, which I have to this day. That was a powerful experience for me, and somewhat cathartic. I still choke up each time I remember it.

Why was I allowed to live when Dave French had to die? That helicopter seat he was in was supposed to be mine. Did he die in my place? Should I not have let Dave make the pay run when he wanted to? Is this helicopter going to go down? Am I going to die in this place?

I was a different man after Vietnam. I thought about that as I waited once again for a helicopter, hoping for a better outcome than my dear friend, Dave French.

Reproduced by permission from the Vietnam Veterans Memorial Fund

David French, my friend and Vietnam roommate. I was blessed to find this picture of him at the Vietnam Memorial.

Chapter 16
A FEEL GOOD STORY
Late August, Early September 2006

Many of my friends thought my whole drowning story should have been reported in the Fresno Bee, our local newspaper, which reports everything worth hearing about. Nobody knew why, but it had slipped under the radar of the reporters, and that was okay with me. I'm not big on notoriety. But after thinking about it for a few weeks, I decided it might make a good story, mainly because all people were reading about were adverse reports, like cancer and car crashes. Wouldn't it be refreshing for people to read or hear about a survival story? I called Don Mayhew, one of the writers at the Bee whose stories I had read over the years. He seemed to be honest and thorough, as near as I could tell, so I hoped he'd be interested.

"Don, I'm pretty sure you haven't heard about my whitewater accident where the CHP brought me to UMC? I was in a coma for about two and a half weeks and hospitalized for about three and a half. It might be a story your readers would like to hear."

"Why are you calling me?" he asked.

"I've read your articles over the years, and you seem to be pretty honest in your reporting," I said.

"Tell me a little about the story."

I related enough of the story to give him a pretty fair outline.

"I can't believe we missed this. Yes, it sounds like something I could do. Where can I meet you?"

I gave him my address. Two days later, he called and said he was coming over. I wasn't expecting him to be punctual, but he was—almost to the minute. When he drove up in his Jeep Cherokee, I could immediately tell he was the kind of reporter who would go just about anywhere, anytime, to get a good story—a "ready for anything" type of guy. I knew I'd called the right reporter/writer, and time proved me right. He didn't waste a second getting down to business.

"Welcome, Don, come in," I said as we shook hands. Still, I was a bit nervous about this. I wanted to get the details right, but I still struggled to remember some things.

"Let's start with where you were and what you were doing."

"My boys, five of them, signed us up to go on a two-day rafting trip with Kings River Expeditions down the Kings River to experience some rapids during the annual snowmelt."

"I've met Jeb and Julie—they run a first-class operation, so you picked a great team. How'd you end up in the hospital?"

"On the second day, we were going through a section of the river known as Bonzai Canyon when our raft flipped. I was swept into a keeper and drowned. The raft ahead of us pulled over and got five of us, but my son Nathan and I were caught up in the keeper. Nathan was thrown out quickly and immediately made it to the bank a little further downriver, out of the water, glad to be alive. When my body came out, they were able to recover it and did twenty-two minutes of CPR. One of the guys had a cell phone and went down the road, closer to the lake, to get cell reception, and he called 911. The helicopter they dispatched thought we were at Trimmer Springs and couldn't find us, but the CHP helicopter found us. Andrea Brown and Paul Dwyer flew me to UMC."

"I know Andrea from reporting on many of their rescues," Don said. "She's got an amazing track record. You lucked out to run into her. Tell me who some of the key people at the hospital were."

"Between Kelly and me, we can tell you that Dr. Usman Javed and Dr. Swarna were key doctors, although there are many more specialists—especially the nurses in the ICU.

"This is great so far. Indeed, I will need to have conversations with the people who worked on your recovery and gather their perspectives. I'm sure this story will blossom into something our readers want to hear. I'm still in shock about how none of my usual sources picked up on this, and it slipped through the cracks. The other thing I want to cover is how your recovery is going! It's one thing for the hospital staff to bring you back and get you on your feet again, but what's recovery like?"

"It was touch and go for a long time in the hospital, and there were a lot of unexpected consequences I had to figure out. For example, being comatose and immobile for three weeks did a number on all the muscles in my body. I'm still amazed at how just that little amount of time would cause me to lose forty pounds of muscle. I can't imagine what it would be like to be confined to a wheelchair or be bedridden for a long time—the muscle loss would be rapid and drastic. But being intubated and incapacitated has affected parts of me that I don't even think about, like my epiglottis! Swallowing fluids was suddenly challenging with 'going down the wrong pipe' happening all the time, causing serious convulsive episodes so severe that I've developed a mild fear of drinking anything in public!"

"Do you need someone to be with you all the time?" Don asked.

"No. My balance and gait are good, and I'm rebuilding pretty well, thanks to the physical therapy department at the VA Hospital. My shoulders and legs seem to have shrunk, but they're coming back with weights and exercises, so I'm hopeful I'll get back to normal. I've never been much of a workout person, so an athletic physique hasn't been on my agenda. But when I was at the gym recently, one of my friends joked, 'Hey Miller, is that you, or are you riding a chicken?' The difference is pretty stark!"

I took him out in my new backyard, which wasn't landscaped at all, so he could see the river where I walk and run for exercise. The view is impressive, and he got the picture. On the other side of our wrought-iron fence is an almost straight down cliff, and at the bottom is a little alluvial bordering the river. It features a sandy trail that many residents and visitors use. And me.

"How do you get down there? Surely you don't slide down two hundred feet in those weeds!" Don looked out over the fence rail again.

"My neighbor has built a staircase, right over there, with halves of railroad ties that go all the way down, and his gardener uses the weed-eater on it, so although it's an arduous climb down and back, it's pretty easy, very much like doing stairs at the football stadium.

But it will get you panting, which is why I do it. I seem to be regaining much of my lung function.

"I'm expecting that you're going to want to talk to the KRE crew, so when you're ready, I can get you phone numbers and names."

"I've already spoken with Jeb, and he has me set up with key people on the rafting side of things who will be glad to help," Don said. "Although they've never had a fatality in thirty-three years, it's a big deal to them that this was almost a first on their watch. A bad review would damage their reputation, so they're glad I'm planning to be discreet."

"That's good news—I think they have an incredible operation, and I wouldn't want to be the one to mess them up. Thanks."

A week later, Don and his photographer met with Thomas, Kevin, and me. We drove up to the Kings River to Bonzai Canyon, where the drowning had occurred. We discussed it on the way, talking about the river's seasons and how we used to come in August and ride air mattresses on it with our five-year-old kids. And we'd spend hours catching crawfish to take home for gumbo. Thomas and I both discussed our military experiences to fill the time, since it's a long drive.

When we got there, the photographer got to work, taking pictures of the area. The water level was way down—probably eight or ten feet lower than during snowmelt—so the tenacity of the Kings was not on display. But it was very easy to imagine it, at least for Thomas, Kevin, and me. For the first time, I could see how deep the keeper was, since the rock that had been redirecting the river was almost completely exposed.

"Hard to believe this could have been so dangerous that it could kill you," Don said. "I'm imagining the water hitting this rock, but a fifteen-foot keeper? Wow. This river must have been a real mother when the snowmelt was full-on. You say you couldn't even see that there was a keeper here?"

"All I saw was surging white water!" I said. "It's amazing what white water covers up. And this whole area around the rock here was submerged. Gives you an idea how high the water was, and that there was no escaping it."

The keeper had been between ten and twenty feet deep, including the gouged riverbed at the base of the rock. We could easily visualize how it had become so powerful. When I stood on the road above Bonzai, I felt a deep respect for the ominous force of nature that had once conquered me, but now I had a second chance at life. And I remembered waking up from the coma in the hospital and the vision I saw on the ceiling. For just a few seconds, I had this feeling that something had happened when I was pulled from the water—something that I should be able to remember but couldn't. And just as quickly as it hit me, it was gone.

From this elevated position, I felt as if God were standing next to me, reminding me that He had brought me through the keeper and was allowing me to share His love for humanity—for me. It wasn't fear, not regret, not anything intense, but the sense of being glad it was time to turn the page. Here in the bright sunlight, from the safety of the road, it wasn't looking so ominous now. I found that amazingly deceptive, as if the "Beast of Bonzai" were hiding under the sand at the base of the big rock, waiting for another snowmelt to release it.

When we returned to Fresno, Don wanted to visit the VA Physical Therapy Department to assess my progress in recovery. That was uneventful, but he was now appreciating the depth of the whole experience. It was a bigger deal than he thought, especially after he'd interviewed Andrea Brown, the CHP EMT. She thought he should write the article!

"I've been on a whole lot of very serious rescues in my twenty-plus years as a CHP EMT in a helicopter, and this has to be one of the best," Andrea told Don Mayhew. "I thought his chances of survival were zip, since he'd been so long in chest compressions, and he was no spring chicken! And he had diabetes and was on insulin! No, the experiences I've had would completely rule out recovery. But today he's breathing, walking, and recovering. Goodness, I can only tell you that God moves in mysterious ways. The only other recovery I had who survived something almost as bad was a paramedic we pulled out of the river, and he wasn't under for very long. We got him back pretty quickly. But this guy? Unreal. We were all blown away."

The four-page article was published in the Sunday edition on September 3, 2006, accompanied by color photos. I hadn't been given a chance to proofread it, but I didn't regret that. It turned out to be a great article. I called the Bee the next week to thank Don, but he had already moved to Florida, where his daughter was attending college.

The article's results were profound. It wasn't so much that the community was looking for someone to shower with accolades, which it was, but that everyone appreciated a "feel-good story" about drowning that had a positive outcome.

Within a matter of a month, I heard from at least a dozen people who had lost someone to drowning, and I was able to explain my experience, which invariably provided some comfort. I explained that once you inhale water, unconsciousness happens almost immediately, especially in my case, where there was no sputtering or choking because my lungs had been empty before I breathed in and filled them with water. When I was able to say that I felt no pain, honestly, many expressed deep relief, able to let go of tortured feelings and regrets.

For example, I was in line at the supermarket one day when a lady I had never met asked me, "Are you that guy in the newspaper article who drowned?" When I averred that I was, she told me her five-year-old son had drowned in their pool, and they didn't discover him until an hour later. She had agonized over losing him, but also felt tremendous guilt for having caused him such a painful death. I told her how painless it is. She didn't believe me at first, but when I explained how quickly the brain shuts down, she felt relieved. Several other shoppers were teary-eyed, too, as they listened to my experience.

I felt blessed to know that God was using my experience to help others; my gratitude that my health was improving every day was also because of Him.

Dr. Behnam continued to monitor my diabetes, my swallowing, and my physical therapy for the next three months. Eventually, my recovery had progressed to the point where I could walk several miles, then jog, and finally run.

When Dr. Behnam rotated to a new assignment after about three months, the VA gave me another "primary doctor," Suneetha Dandala. I had improved enough that I didn't need regular monitoring or any special attention, so I only saw her about every six months after that. The VA is very good at monitoring veterans, and their records are thorough; however, I sometimes had issues with how they handled us. I was not a whiner, but I second-guessed most of their dictums. I needed to know what was causing the problems, what the prognosis was, and what alternatives were being suggested. But I got along well with Dr. Dandala.

Now that I was back in the real world and my ARDS wasn't slowing me down, I wanted to find out if I had, indeed, suffered some cognitive damage. I had Dr. Dandala refer me to a psychiatric clinic, where I could be tested. The doctor there primarily worked with veterans who were experiencing age-related issues, like Alzheimer's, so that's where we started. The initial tests focused on identifying squares and circles and determining their similarities. I handled it pretty easily, although I was amazingly unskilled in drawing.

When I was done, he graded it and told me to "Get outta here! You're in the ninety percentiles, and I don't see anything wrong with you that won't disappear when you get your musculature back." That was good news because I was afraid there were some hidden potholes in my head that would need to be addressed as I continued to recover.

After all those weeks of wondering if I would make it and all of the ups and downs, I overheard Kelly saying this to someone on the phone about me: "From the moment he woke up in the hospital, Thom was happy to be still alive, and he sure didn't have an 'I'm just going to sit here and vegetate' attitude," she said. "That was not his motivation. He recognized that he had work to do and needed to improve to accomplish it. We moved him out of the store and home to work, so we brought his work stuff home. When he was ready to work again, he did it here at home. He did not doubt that he would work again.

We made him walk up and down the stairs, and it was hard at first. Still, he put all he could into it every day."

I smiled at her kind words. When she hung up the phone, I grabbed her and gave her a big hug of appreciation.

Chapter 17
MAKING NEW MEMORIES
Mid-October 2006

The week after I got out of the hospital, there was another drowning on the lower portion of the Kings River below the dam. A woman had let her child go into the river to get wet, and he'd gone out over his head and began floundering. She jumped in to get him, but couldn't swim. A bystander retrieved the child, who was okay, but when they pulled her out, she wasn't breathing. They did CPR, and she was revived after several minutes. The EMTs came with the ambulance, and she was taken to the hospital. The paper reported it as another person saved by CPR from drowning, but a week later, her obituary was printed—she didn't make it after all. Indeed, as my doctors had pointed out, drowning and the recovery from it are very complicated.

One of our local television stations has a program called "Med Watch," which highlights amazing experiences involving interventions and recoveries. It's all about encouraging and appreciating the work that our medical professionals do every day. They brought their production team to my home for a short interview with my whole family, which was the first time I'd heard my boys talk about what they experienced! It was almost traumatic for me to listen to it all.

We sat on a large couch in the living room, with the boys standing behind us, while the moderator—Mary Lisa Russell—asked questions of each of us, but mostly me. I began with the first-time rafting experience, and Thomas described the water level and how cold it was.

"Most of the year, the Kings River is just a stream, but when the snowpacks melt, it becomes a raging beast for about six weeks and is great for rafting," Thomas said. "We enjoyed it until Dad went into the keeper. After we recovered him and did CPR for twenty-two minutes, it was another ninety minutes before the CHP helicopter came and took him to UMC. Doctors told us it was a miracle he survived that long."

"And Thom, what were you thinking while all this was happening?"

"I wasn't there! I don't know where I was, but it wasn't with these guys. I have no recollection of this."

The moderator asked a few more questions to paint a picture of the entire event, and then the gang walked with him into the kitchen, resuming their discussion of the drowning while standing around the island.

"My biggest concern was fishing him out of the river!" Michael said. "I had a picture of him going downstream and getting stuck in the brush or something, and if that happened, it was 'turn out the lights, the party's over.'"

"I was still freaked out, since I went a cycle in the keeper, too, and I was lucky to get out," Nathan said. "I swam as hard as I could to reach the bank. I saw Dad come out of Bonzai, and I knew he was done. I had the feeling that could have been me." That was the first time I'd heard that Nathan saw me come out of the keeper.

Tim joined the conversation. "The daily news from the doctors was somewhat encouraging, but never really positive like we were expecting. In the end, I think they realized this is a God thing, and medicine, as best they could apply it, wasn't the whole answer. Yeah, they did amazing and relentless treatment, but he recovered beyond their expectations, and quicker than anyone had imagined. I had a great time keeping up with the terminology and procedures, so much so that I'm thinking of getting into nursing."

"When Mom and I got to the hospital and they ushered us into 'the quiet room,' I was not feeling very good about it," Elizabeth shared. "To be there waiting to hear about Dad was almost too much—so much goes through your mind that you're ready to start crying any minute."

"I had never heard of a Level One Trauma Center," I said. It was interesting to discover that Fresno's UMC is one of the few such facilities in California. And a RotoRest bed, which is required equipment for recovering drowning victims, is readily available—I'd never heard of such a machine! See these bald spots on the back of my head, behind my ears—when they strapped me on the bed, they had to also strap my head down on pads, and now hair won't grow there. Barbers always want to know what happened, thinking maybe I'm afflicted with alopecia and might have cooties or something."

We continued like that, each one of us sharing our own perspectives on the event. It was nice, but I think we all realized how traumatized we had been.

They aired that interview probably every other week for most of a year, and we still saw it on occasion, even years later. I suppose that's because it was popular, and it truly stands out as a testament to the dedication of the ICU doctors and staff.

The American Red Cross presents an annual Hero Award for various incidents, and my near-drowning was nominated for the Wilderness Award. The article came out in the Sunday edition of the Fresno Bee. On Monday morning, I received a call from Rebecca with the Central Valley Chapter of the Red Cross, who asked me questions about the accident.

"So, are you a swimmer and just had a bad day, or was this a complete surprise for you?"

"Actually," I said, "I've got all the water event Scout merit badges and was almost at Life level before I had to drop out. I was on a swimming team before high school. No, this keeper was a complete shock to me. It was hidden in the surging white water and got me totally by surprise."

When she determined that I was the real deal, she asked if I'd like to nominate "my team" for the Wilderness Award, which would be awarded soon. Each winner would have their own gala awards dinner. Of course, I said, "Aw, sure!"

We won the competition, and there was a huge dinner and award ceremony featuring my sons, my brother Gordie, Kevin Davis, and the CHP officers. All the political dignitaries signed the award certificates—the governor, senators, members of Congress from our region, the mayor, and others—and the truly official plaques could be mounted on desks and walls. Nathan even has his mounted in his law office. It was quite distinguishing and impressive. The Master of Ceremonies, Rich Rodriguez, who was and is a popular local TV newscaster, knew all of us and made it very personal—we were all the more awed! It was a powerful event that we'll never forget.

Not long afterward, I received a call from a nurse at Valley Children's Hospital asking me to visit a child who had a traumatic water experience and was afraid of the water now. Ostensibly, I was to give him the courage not to fear the water, but instead to respect it and become more familiar with his limitations. I just needed to renew his commitment to enjoying water experiences again.

This child, Bobby, was about seven, with curly dishwater blonde hair, large blue eyes, and freckles across his nose. He was lanky and maybe tall for his age, but he didn't look like it, as he seemed to shrink himself into his bed. He seemed pretty traumatized, although he was there for observation, not treatment. He hadn't been in the water long and had no real damage to his lungs. Still, he was quiet, shy, and only nodded yes or no at me.

"Bobby, I hear you had a run-in with some water you weren't ready for. Sounds like it was pretty harrowing! I had a similar experience not very long ago, and I've got to tell you, it was scary—even for me."

His eyes were wide and expressive as he nodded.

I told him about my Scout merit badges and how much work it took to earn them, but in the end, I felt at ease in the water. "But you know, we're not fish or seals or other water creatures. When we're in the water, sometimes it feels like we're comfortable in it, but don't let that fool you. You have to constantly be aware that one little slip could deprive you of the air you need to survive. But with practice—maybe training—you could become an expert, like a Navy SEAL (Sea, Air, and Land)! Do you know who they are?"

Again, he nodded, this time scooting up to sit a little higher and leaning in toward me.

"They go through extreme training and are considered to be the best of the best in the Navy, like the Army's Green Berets. They're experts in swimming in all kinds of conditions, even rough seas in the ocean. When you're older, you might want to check it out, as they love sharing what they do with young people interested in pursuing the same path. Just remember, enjoy time swimming and playing in the water, but always keep your guard up because it's easy to get distracted and get hurt when you're in unfamiliar water."

It was a new challenge for me, and I'm not sure how convincing I was. I gave it my best "dad" shot. However, while I was there, I met two nurses who were familiar with my story. One was the mother of the rafter Bill, who ran down the road and made the 911 call. She was genuinely sorry about the location mix-up, but I was adamant that he was a big part of my miracle, and I am forever grateful for his efforts. The other nurse was one of the trauma nurses on the 911 chopper, and she hadn't heard about the CHP extraction until Don Mayhew's article was published in the Bee. She said she and several other nurses were still anguishing about their inability to find us.

A member of the Optimists Club asked me to share my experience at his monthly meeting. I didn't fancy myself a speaker and was reluctant, but happily agreed to share. The thirty-minute presentation went okay. But one of the big questions I always get is, "After you died, did you see the light?" I had to confess that I didn't remember anything after I inhaled water. I had thought that was normal, since I'd been given a ton of Versed in the hospital, which is a painkiller, but it also wipes out your short-term memory. I didn't expect to have any real memories of the time that I was technically dead. However, I did wonder why I survived when the odds were so slim. If I could remember what happened, maybe I would have that question answered.

When I was revived, I remembered coughing up water, sitting up, telling the boys to help me up, and saying, "I'll walk it off." I could recall not being able to breathe on the way to the hospital. And when

I finally became conscious in the hospital, I could remember several weird and intense dreams, almost nightmares, while I was unconscious. One of those dreams was an extremely vivid picnic, where I found myself in a grassy park near a river, listening to Dennis Weaver tell a story to a crowd of picnickers. I was reclining in the grass below the knoll where he was walking and talking, in his unique voice, and I watched his cowboy boots as he walked by. I thought he was telling the story to me, and all the other people were listening to his monologue. Later, I found out that Dennis Weaver had died three months before my accident. It was such a strange dream.

After taking a few questions from the Optimists and wrapping up the presentation, I was getting ready to leave when one of the men in the audience approached me. He introduced himself, and we began an intriguing conversation.

"I have a recommendation for you about the memory lapse," he said. "But let me explain first. When you're alive, your body and your soul are one. The memories of events reside in both. But when you die, your body loses its memory. The neurons that comprise the brain cease to function. When you're dead, there's no way your brain can generate any memories at all. But your soul does. If you can access your soul's memory, the problem is solved. How? Therapy. I've heard it works very well. I know a woman who is one of the top therapists in the state for this type of thing. I'll get you her info if you're interested."

"Okay, I'm open to checking it out. I'm pretty much a hard-core, closed-minded guy, but who knows? If I could get to the bottom of where I was during the twenty-two minutes of CPR, it would answer a lot of my questions and maybe stop the nagging feelings of almost remembering something."

It could also create a massive package of questions I hadn't even considered.

He called me that evening with the doctor's phone number, and I called her the following week.

As I picked up the phone to place the call, I was reminded of an event that had taken place decades earlier, when I wondered why I had survived against all odds. It’s a fantastic story that changed my life.

Chapter 18
FLASHBACK: WHERE'S CHARLIE?
1967

Back in 1967, I had extended my tour in Vietnam and performed well in G-3. I enjoyed teaming up with the officers and, eventually, with the E-9 sergeant major, with whom I worked daily. We respected each other and collaborated efficiently. I had progressed through the ranks pretty quickly and was promoted to E-5 within twelve months. My superiors seemed pleased that I had made some improvements in our procedures in G-3 and was on the list for a pro-pay increase and a rank promotion to E-6.

One of my duties was to manage the G-3 Jeep, ensuring that the officers and my sergeant major had it available whenever needed. I would drive it from our MACV Compound in Qui Nhon every day, about fifteen kilometers—a little more than nine miles—to BaGi, the ARVN 22nd Division HQ, where we spent our days.

The carpenters would soon finish a batch of "hooches" being built for the advisors, but for now, we drove to Qui Nhon every day. BaGi was an assembly of bare warehouses converted into offices, probably originally built by the French, with corrugated tin roofs. The facility was very austere, but functional, and we fit in pretty well. I particularly enjoyed it when we had the regular pelting rainstorms that made loud music on the roof! Then we drove back to Qui Nhon whenever we were done for the day, between 4:00 and 6:00 p.m.

Right next to BaGi was a small hill, about a thousand feet high, popping up out of nowhere on the edge of the flat plain of Binh Dinh Province. Rice paddies stretched for miles on the fertile flat plain between the mountains of the Central Highlands and the sea. It was a unique landmark. On the summit of this flat-topped hill stood the ancient "Banh It Cham Temple," built in the late 12th and early 13th centuries by the people of the Champa Kingdom, who worshipped Hindu gods. It was constructed of red bricks in a circular structure with a diameter of approximately fifty feet, resembling a teepee, with an opening located about fifty feet up at the center. The interior had a hard, dirt floor with an open doorway on both sides, marked by the evidence of smoke from old fires within. I think the local Vietnamese were afraid of the spirits there and considered the temple taboo because they never went up there.

The circular road leading to the top of the hill was relatively narrow and steep, and next to the "temple" was a flat space suitable for parking a Jeep or two. The US 1st Cav Division had a liaison officer attached to the 22nd ARVN, who worked through our G-3, and had a communications Jeep parked at the temple, loaded with powerful radio equipment and a generator. They had radio antennae mounted outside, next to the temple. The sergeant stationed at the temple, SSG Hollis Reasons, had set up the radios inside and maintained direct radio contact with me in G-3, about a mile away. We shared intel on troop locations and operations and became friends.

When Sgt. Reasons' tour was over, and he was scheduled to go home, the 1st Cav sent a chopper to our helipad with a special load of supplies for him, which included some mighty fine steaks. He invited me to a barbecue on his last night to celebrate with him. Sgt. Reasons confessed to me that he had the heebie-jeebies being there all alone, that something spiritual was going on. I didn't feel it.

He had invited me up there a few months earlier to watch operations develop as the 22nd fought with NVA attackers stealing rice from our nearby villagers. From there, we watched "Puff" rain hell on an NVA company which had crossed Highway One—the main road separating the rice paddies from the sea—and was in full combat mode. Puff, initially called "Spooky," was a C-47 twin-engine troop carrier—modified DC-3-with three electric mini-cannons mounted in a doorway on the left side, allowing it to bank left and circle to focus fire on a small area. It took a crew of six airmen to keep the weapons constantly loaded. The rate of fire was unbelievable. Every seventh round was a red tracer, and there were three cannons firing. Puff was pretty new, and Sgt: Reasons figured I'd enjoy seeing it in action.

"Thom, look straight over there where the gunfire is happening," he said. "That's all NVA noise because the village there is probably deserted by now—they don't have any protection. I see this happening twice a week, but you can't put ARVN troops everywhere."

"Yeah, I know," I said. "They still have to have sweep and search-and-destroy missions to be effective in interdicting the NVA, so trying to focus on one attack is not practical. I'm just glad we have the 22nd Recon platoon guarding BaGi because otherwise those hungry bad guys could try to overrun the HQ here."

He nodded. "One of the advisors attached to the 41st Regiment, Sgt. Deedy, who controls this area, called in Puff—I heard the call earlier, so I knew this was coming. I'm gonna requisition some popcorn from the 1st Cav before I leave because this'll be happening more and more! See if you don't think this is movie-quality! Keep watching."

The view from the temple was spectacular, and we listened to the radio traffic as the fight unfolded and quickly ended. As the plane circled, we could see a solid stream of red. To add to the incredible "shock and awe" it inspired, the eerie roar of the aircraft and its cannons, which oscillated as it banked, was something else. The whole event was frightening! Very quickly, it became known as Puff the Magic Dragon, a popular song at the time by Peter, Paul, and Mary, and the NVA had no idea what was happening as it chewed up their entire unit. A sweep operation after the fighting stopped was productive—many of the NVA survivors were severely frightened. Our G-2 interrogators told me the troops we captured were sure it was a real dragon, and they were doomed.

On the evening of the BBQ, I headed up to the temple while it was still light, probably about 5:00 p.m. It was the start of monsoon season, and when the winds picked up and brought rain, it would come in buckets, practically horizontal, and probably last all night. Sgt. Reasons and I were protected inside the temple, so we didn't notice it developing as we were having a good time barbecuing steaks, drinking Jack Daniels, and listening to radio conversations from all around the world. With his robust radios, he could even tune in to discussions in Europe.

"Betty, is that you? Over."

"Well, Robert, it's not your mother! I'm sure missing you tonight, and I wish you'd bring some joy home soon! Over."

"Yeah, honey, I do have a lot of joy that I'm bringing home next week. I hope you're ready for it."

Conversations like this were on many channels, and as we drank Jack, we laughed about our bad fortune in not having anyone we could call.

I finally noticed the changing weather and said good night, since it was about 9:00 p.m. I jumped in my Jeep, which had no top on it, and headed down the hill for a usually thirty-minute, fifteen-kilometer drive into Qui Nhon. The wind picked up almost immediately, and I was just in time to head into the heavy rain, which was slanted—nearly horizontal—and coming straight at me. Fortunately, it wasn't coming from my side because I was unprotected. If I were attacked and had to protect myself, I would need to have an unobstructed field of view to fire in any direction. G-2 had shared, earlier that day, reports of a Viet Cong platoon in the area robbing rice from villagers. The enemy was most active during inclement weather because that's when we couldn't use artillery and aircraft on them. I didn't have my PRC-25 radio with me, which I usually had in the Jeep, but this drive was so routine that I hadn't expected to need it. If it had been field operations, I would have carried it on my back to communicate with aircraft, artillery, or other units. As it was, it wouldn't have helped me anyway because there weren't any friendly units operating during the storm.

In no time, I discovered how bad this whole idea was. My headlights were nearly useless in the heavy rain, so I had to slow down quite a bit to see the road at all. Highway One is a one-lane road in each direction, with no centerline and is plagued by numerous potholes due to heavy truck traffic.

In one of the easy S turns, snaking between the rice paddies, I must have overcorrected when I hit a pothole and lost traction on the slick highway. I careened out of control, spinning in a circle and off the road, and plunged about four feet into a rice paddy, nose first. When the Jeep hit bottom in the shallow paddy, about two feet of water deep, the front of it was bent, and the hood buckled. My face hit the steering wheel, and I was knocked out. The Jeep rolled twice, and I was thrown out the right side, along with the passenger seat and my rifle that had been on it.

When I recovered consciousness, I was on my back in the rice paddy with my face just out of the water and blood all over.

This is not good. Will the Jeep even run now? Thank God the headlights are still working! And if I can get it going—are you serious? There's no way. Where's Charlie? How am I going to make it back to Qui Nhon? This storm is vicious, and where am I?

I have no idea what kept my face out of the water because it was at least two feet deep where I landed. The Jeep was on its right side, balanced six inches next to me, teetering. Fortunately, I wasn't pinned under it and was able to roll away and stand up. I pushed the Jeep forward with one hand, and it rolled back onto all four wheels. I got in, turned the engine over, and it started! The headlights were still on, so I could see what had happened and what I had to do to get back on the road. So I shifted the transmission into low gear and drove out of the water, up the four-foot edge of the paddy, and onto the road. The first surge up the embankment failed, and I slid back. But I went a little slower the second time to get more traction in the wet dirt.

The fan blades were hitting something, making quite a racket, but my concern was to make it the next mile or two into town before something blew up. The radiator wasn't cooling the engine, so it was hissing loudly as I slowly drove. Both lights were aimed up at the sky at forty-five degrees, like beacons, which frightened me because the noise and the lights were making me a target. Above the din of the driving wind and the buckets of rain, I was visible, if there were any bad guys nearby. The road was almost invisible, so I had to go very slowly. After about ten minutes, I reached the edge of town.

There was an MP—military police from the USARV (United States Army, Vietnam) maintenance battalion stationed in Qui

Nhon—blockade, and the curfew had been 6:00 p.m. However, MACV personnel were exempt from curfew because we could visit our counterparts anywhere in the countryside. Indeed, that happened occasionally.

"Halt. Stop the vehicle and exit, hands up."

"Okay, I'm headed to the MACV Compound on the other side of town—"

"I'm talking. When I want you to talk, I'll tell you." The MP was an E-5 sergeant, the same rank as me, so I was a little miffed at the lack of respect.

"Now, what are you doing out here?"

"I'm coming from the Division HQ at BaGi, fifteen klicks up Highway One. I slid off the road a few klicks back and crashed in a rice paddy, and I'm late getting back to my unit—"

"Get in our Jeep. I'm arresting you for being out after curfew. And you smell like alcohol is involved, so you'll have to be jailed until someone can come escort you to your unit."

"You can see from the patch on my pocket here that I'm with MACV—"

"Get into the Jeep and shut up."

I smelled like Jack Daniels, so they immediately impounded my Jeep, arrested me, and took me to their compound and jail. I was put in with a bunch of drunks from the maintenance battalion who had been partying in town and fighting. The duty officer, a second lieutenant, called our MACV Compound and figured they'd send somebody from guard duty to pick me up. But our G-3 Assistant, Captain Wilburn Boozer (a West Point grad), showed up. He was a great example of a sharp officer, and I appreciated working for him. He was shaking his head at me, but Capt. Boozer sure was impressive as he marched me out after giving the MPs some choice words for imprisoning me.

"You realize you have no authority to arrest MACV personnel, and you should have driven him to our unit! Next time, do the right thing, or we'll be having words with your commanding officer! And Miller, will there be a next time?"

"No, sir." We drove the five minutes back to the compound quietly, and I thanked him for helping me out. I was subdued the next day in G-3.

The jeep wasn't a total loss—the engine was okay, and the rest was repaired pretty quickly.

The next morning at about 8:00 a.m., Sergeant Major Higgins and I borrowed the G-2 jeep and drove out to the location where it happened. The right seat from my jeep was still there, about fifty feet out in the paddy.

"Miller, you are one lucky SOB. How the hell that seat could have been flung out that far is a mystery to me. You must have been going forty miles an hour when you slid off the road! Go on out there, grab that seat, and let's get out of here."

"No, honestly, I was only going about ten miles an hour! I'm on it, though. Maybe I can even find my weapon out there." I didn't want to get into any further trouble.

Right next to the seat, and under two feet of water, I quickly located my M-2 carbine—I was relieved to know that someone had not already found it. My nickname—radio call sign—became Crash 3 that day. The third was because I was in G-3.

I was pleased that I wasn't reprimanded with an Article 15, which is typically the disciplinary action taken for driving under the influence and wrecking a military vehicle. It involved a reduced pay grade to E-4 and a fine. They removed me from the promotion and pro-pay lists. Enough said.

This adventure is significant because when I came to after the crash and was lying next to the jeep with my face just barely out of the water—that alone was miraculous—I would have been crushed and drowned if the jeep had continued to roll. One more roll and my head would have been submerged. The extent of my injuries was a badly bruised nose and bruising to my shoulder, but I had no broken bones. It shocked me that the Jeep's engine fired up right away. That and the fact that the vehicle threw me out and stopped before crushing me is meaningful. As it was, it took almost no effort for me to push it back onto its wheels, which meant it was precariously balanced after it came to a stop.

Furthermore, I was all alone, knocked out, and no one knew where I was or would have thought to come looking for me until the next morning. To top it off, G-2 had shared intelligence with me the day before that an enemy company was raiding the nearby hamlets. I was amazed and blessed to have been able to sneak past them.

I wondered why I survived that crash when so many of my fellow soldiers died in Vietnam. I could only surmise that it was just not my time to go.

Chapter 19
TWENTY-TWO MINUTES
Mid-October 2006

As the phone rang, and I waited to make an appointment with the therapist, the thought struck me that once again, it had not been my time to go when I drowned in the King's River, just as it hadn't been when Dave French died in the helicopter crash instead of me, and when I crashed in the rice paddy. But I truly wanted to know what happened to me when I was dead for twenty-two minutes. I realized it had been haunting me. I hoped this would help.

A pleasant voice answered my call. "This is Susan. How may I help you?"

"Doctor, I've been referred to you to help me resolve an issue that's been plaguing me. I was in an accident and then hospitalized, and it appears that I could have been dead as long as twenty-five minutes before I was revived. I want to find out where I was during those twenty-two to twenty-five minutes that I was dead. Can you help me recover the memory? "

She was silent for a few moments, perhaps gathering her thoughts. When she finally responded, her voice was clear and kind.

"Call me Susan. Tell me about your accident and why you think I can help. I understand what you're looking for, but this is a little unusual."

"I was in a whitewater accident where the boat flipped, and I was swept into something called a keeper. A few cycles in, I ended up inhaling an entire lungful of water. I vividly remember reaching for the surface and then being pulled down, and then I have no memory until they revived me about thirty minutes later. I want to know what happened during the time they were doing CPR on me. The man who referred me to you told me that the soul and the body share the same memory while you're alive, but the soul retains a memory of what happens after you're dead. When your body and soul come together again, as in my case, you can access the soul's memory through therapeutic practices. Is this true?"

"That's a succinct description of what happens, and I do believe I can help. It works for some people, and for some it doesn't," she said. "You are an eager patient, so I expect good results with you. Why don't you come to my office tomorrow morning at ten, and we'll see? It will take about an hour."

After I hung up, I felt encouraged and hopeful, even excited, that the experience would be fruitful, but I had no idea what it would be like.

This is going to be interesting. I'm tired of these nagging thoughts that I'm missing something. I should be able to remember it all. I've healed up well, and my mind is intact. I need to know more about what happened to me.

Her office was not glamorous. The room was small, with a comfortable, table-like bed—similar to an ER bed—on which I lay.

Susan was tall and thin, with short, bobbed, blond hair and small but kind eyes. She was pleasant, rather stoic, and serious. She asked me if I was nervous and sure that I wanted to go forward with this, and I said, "Absolutely! What do I have to lose?"

She smiled, sat in a chair next to me, and turned on a recording device, which I had agreed to in the paperwork I signed upon arrival.

She spoke softly but confidently. "Thom, I want you to relax. First your hands, then your arms and legs, then your eyes. Breathe deeply and slowly. Work on this for a few minutes, and you should be relaxed. You should feel no stress on your face."

Before I knew it, I was so relaxed that I wondered if I'd fall asleep. It felt sort of like that state we're in just as we're falling asleep.

"When you are relaxed like this, it's easiest for you to remember events," Susan said. "As you recall things, I will prompt you to tell me what's happening, and then I will ask you to move on to the next memory. I won't suggest anything to you because your memory needs to speak for itself."

I understood fully what she was saying to me, but I didn't feel the need to respond. I felt so comfortable and peaceful.

"Now, picture yourself rafting on the river, approaching the spot where the raft flipped you out. Then, when you're ready, I want you to remember what it was like when you first hit the water. Then I want you to remember exactly what it felt like to be in the water." She paused for a moment. "Okay, where are you? What do you feel?"

"I'm swimming in the whitewater. It's cold. My wetsuit isn't helping. I'm freezing. And the water is so strong. It's too powerful for me. I can't control it." I responded to her as she guided me. My arms were covered in serious goosebumps—I was feeling the icy water. This was incredibly real.

"What do you feel as you get closer to the keeper?"

"I'm desperate. The water's too much for me, and I want to get out. I'm reaching for the rock with a rough ledge so I can pull up on it to get out. Oh no. It's pulling me down. I'm going under, and I can't help myself. I have to hold my breath."

"What are you doing now? What are you thinking?" she asked.

As she questioned me, it was as if she were speaking to me through earphones because I'm hearing her, but I'm focused on what's happening to my body. That scene demanded that I focus. My conversation with her was subdued and relaxed, devoid of the intense emotion I was feeling and concentrating on, as if I were watching a TV or video, experiencing this river scene before me.

"Talk to me, Thom."

"It's pulling me down from my feet and then pushing me up for the third time. It's very powerful and controlling me, and I'm helpless. I'm surging toward the surface, which I can see just above my head. I'm going to let out all my air so that I can take a deeper breath when I pop out this time. Oh my God. No! It's pulling me down before I can get a breath. I'm inhaling water."

"Thom?"

"Everything is black."

She waited a minute before speaking again. "Where are you now?" she asked.

In my mind, I looked around me. "I'm in a very relaxed, very comfortable, and very bright place. Not a room—there are no walls, no floor, and no ceiling that I can see, just a space that I'm in. A very bright white light is flooding my entire field of vision. It's so bright, I can't see anything. But it doesn't hurt my eyes. It's pleasant. I feel like I'm standing in a doorway, but I'm not standing on anything. There's gentle, soft music playing throughout the space, and it's relaxing. Like a Moog synthesizer, though without a melody—just very gentle, smooth, mellow harmonics.

"I feel like the music is going through me, making me feel relaxed, which I'm grateful for because I can't see my body. I think it's here, but I can't see it."

"Where do you think it is?" Susan asked.

"I think I've been transported to the other side. That just now occurred to me out of nowhere. Suddenly, I have no questions. All those questions that had been ebbing to the surface in my thoughts have become moot! I feel as if I've gotten a huge download of answers, information—or maybe it's understanding—and I understand the theoretical and practical issues that I've been puzzled about all my life. It's total understanding. The feeling is amazing, as if God is showing me, without actually showing me, all things. I understand everything about infinity, God, life, and death. It's as if there's no reason to question anything because the answers are already in my mind! The overpowering presence of God the Creator is everywhere, making me feel very, very comfortable, happy, and at peace. I am completely at ease. And extremely awed."

"Okay, tell me about that." I could hear Susan, but I didn't see her.

"I also have an overwhelming and overpowering sense of pure and all-encompassing love, which is so strong and so pervasive that I have no words to express it adequately. I feel joy from this pure love, but it's not from someone, but rather as though God was bathing me in His perfect peace: no conflicts, no regrets, no second thoughts, just comfort and peace all around me.

"I'm thinking about unfinished business, stuff in my garage that nobody would know how to use, records in my office that weren't organized—it seems an overwhelming hassle to leave my family with all that. But now I'm dismissing it all because I know, truly know, the Father will take care of it and take care of my family. I can't worry about it any longer because this love I'm feeling is obliterating anything negative."

"That sounds lovely. Are you still comfortable?" Susan's voice was purely soft and kind.

"I am becoming adjusted to this bright white light and the reality that I can't see anything in it—just this soft, bright whiteness. But wait, seven or eight figures are approaching me. I can't tell who or what they are because the bright light is also like a white fog around me, and I can't see them clearly. They are like electric shadows, sizzling silently like a mirage in a hot desert."

I quit talking for a moment as I was very intrigued by these figures.

"Oh, wait, now I know who they are, and they all recognize me, even though there are no faces and no names here. Just a 'knowing,' which I find heavenly because it cuts through all the 'Hi, how are you?' stuff we are used to on earth. The brightness in the room isn't changing as I'm aware of the presence of these spirits, so I am still somewhat blinded by the light."

"Can you tell me who they are now?" Susan asked.

"It's not that I know them on earth—I can't place where I know them from—nevertheless, I have this feeling that if the fog were to lift, and they were in bodily form, I would be able to recognize them. Yet I know them. It's the craziest thing. They're affectionately greeting me, welcoming me, loving me, expressing gladness that I'm "back"—no names, no faces, only personal love. I'm rejoicing with them, and we are loving each other while having intense conversations, all at the same time! All at once, I feel like I've known them forever. We are closer than family if that's possible. These conversations seem so natural. I don't want to try to figure it out. It's just so wonderful. I'm having eight conversations simultaneously, and it's normal and easy—not one bit confusing."

"Are you excited? What are you feeling?" Susan asked.

"I'm so happy to be with them again. I'm overjoyed, overflowing with love and gladness. And no mouths are moving. I don't even see mouths. It seems to be telepathic communication. So strange, yet natural to me now.

"Several of them want to hear about my life 'down there' and my family, what I've gotten to do in my life. They have lots of questions about my family, like what my children are doing and whether they are good kids—that kind of thing. This back-and-forth dialogue with them is filled with affection and passionate emotions, and I'm loving it. It feels good to be with them again. Although that sounds strange now, it doesn't feel that way to me. There is a powerful feeling of family here, like we have been together before, and I've been away.

"Funny, they're not asking about my career. We're only discussing relationships, feelings, love, and family. The love I share with friends and family is much more important than social status and accomplishments.

"I'm in the midst of one of many conversations, and amazingly, one of them is approaching me, coming much closer than the others. The fog between us has lifted just enough for me to see her. Oh my God! It's my sister Rosemary's daughter, Joanna! She's exactly as I remember her."

"You're with your niece?" Susan asked gently.

"My niece, Joanna Hellwig, was killed in a car wreck five years ago. She had just gotten her driver's license and was taking her sister, Libby, from Exeter to Visalia, a fifteen-minute drive. On a country road, she pulled out from a stop sign and was broadsided by a cement truck that had no stop sign. She died instantly. Libby was injured but recovered fairly quickly. Joanna was a very lovely girl with a big heart, loved by all who knew her. We, her huge family, were all heartbroken."

"I'm so sorry," Susan said. "How are you feeling about this?"

"I do not understand how she can assume human form, or for that matter, how I appear to her—I think we're both spirits—but she's putting her arms around my neck and very gently saying something. 'Uncle Thom, I love you very much, but it's not your time to be part of the oneness. You have to go back and love your family.'

"I'm about to utter a complaint about that, but can't—I'm suddenly back in my freezing body with Thomas doing compressions on my chest. It hurts! I'm moaning in pain."

"Okay, Thom, open your eyes now. Stay relaxed, and let's talk about what you experienced. How do you feel?"

"I'm beyond amazed," I said. My eyes were filled with tears, and I was trembling slightly. "It was incredible. That was a whole different world, and it was so genuine. I don't understand the interdimensionality of it, but maybe that's something God can explain to me someday. It wasn't part of the information I received when I arrived in heaven; I can only call it a download. I was surprised to learn about them, but I don't have any names for them. It was purely a knowing."

"It is real, and I'm glad you were able to do this so easily," Susan said. "That was incredible. Many people can't relax enough to let their minds go. You did well." She explained that there is no "time," as we know it, on the other side, and that spirits are not confined by many of the limitations we identify with, such as names. "Time is a dimension God gives us for our earthly experience. And our names help eliminate a lot of confusion when we don't have telepathy. I've heard of the multi-dimensional telepathic conversations, and I'm glad you experienced it."

I thought about the download and realized I no longer remembered what all I "knew." It was gone. That was a bummer, but I still felt the peace of knowing whatever it was God had shown me.

I wanted to have a more extended conversation with Susan because I had many more questions. It seemed a lot had happened between the time I breathed in the river water and took my first breath after CPR. This foray into a place where people don't go was almost more than I could handle alone, pushing the limits of my imagination.

But my hour was up, and she had only allotted me one hour. Perhaps I could come back someday.

I was still shaking a bit when I left, pondering all I had seen, heard, and felt. I considered going back, but decided I wanted to reflect on this precious experience for a little while.

My niece Joanna Hellwig, not long before she died in a vehicle accident. Seeing her in heaven was one of the most precious moments of my life.

Chapter 20
LOVE RECEIVED AND GIVEN
Mid-October 2006

This whole experience in heaven had blown me away. I wasn't expecting to discover a conduit to the other side, and it was a bit overwhelming. To speak with Joanna, to see her and touch her, was almost more than I could deal with. However, I also felt overjoyed, delighted, and at peace knowing that my perception of the event could be verified. To understand that God allowed me to reconnect with loved ones and communicate with them, and then revel in the experience, was truly elating. Praise God!

After spending a little more than an hour with the therapist, I needed to decompress and reflect on what had happened. God was sending me a directive through Joanna, and I needed to figure this out. If he were leaving me here, perhaps there's a new attitude I should discover and explore from a different perspective. And possibly doing a change like this was going to take a complete reboot of my personal "raison d'être." I was feeling apprehensive, as if I'd opened a box that belonged to Pandora. However, I was also very excited about discovering a new chapter in my life—one I could explore with my family!

Several questions were building in my mind, and I needed to dig a little deeper. For example, in the discussions I had with the spirits who greeted me, I felt that I absolutely had known *all* of them *forever*, intimately, and they had likewise known me. I felt like I was *returning*, and indeed, the conversations we had intimated that. My soul apparently knew these things, and it felt normal while I was there, but now that it's united with my body, I'm wondering how to think about it. To the best of my understanding—and I am not adamant about this, it may change—after God creates our souls, we live in a heavenly environment until He chooses an earthly experience for us and moves us into a physical body. It makes sense now that I know others who know me and are still there.

The most powerful takeaway from the experience was the overwhelming love I received and the love I gave—pure, unconditional love. We're told in Scripture to love each other as we love ourselves, as God loves us, and I was allowed to experience what that's like. It was the real deal. The instruction, through Joanna, was that I needed to love my family. Providing for them and discipling them are part of loving them, but this command shed new light on the whole process and gave me a more profound sense of insight and purpose. I can understand how easy it is to get off track when I'm not following an edict or mandate, but now I remember He's watching me. I already knew that! But I didn't focus on it. And I get the feeling there will be an accounting for it! Much of what I'm experiencing in my new life must be viewed in light of this directive.

I decided to take Joanna's words at face value—that it wasn't my time to join the oneness—and that must be what we consider heaven, where God is. Oneness would imply that we are all joined together there, in one mind with God. The further implication was that I would eventually go to heaven, but first, I had to go back and love my family, and that was a fairly direct instruction—nothing else to read into that except that I had more work to do.

Some of my conclusions were: After death, there is a place our souls go to be "part of the oneness with God." And on this side, God works directly in our lives. He also gives us guardians— sometimes called guardian angels—and, when needed, God uses them to watch over us. I had never given any thought to identifying actions that I should attribute to God's intervention through angels until my hand grabbed the rope. I haven't yet determined the limits of angels' active efforts, but I am now unequivocally aware of their presence. For example, when my hand grabbed the rope as I floated down the river, I was dead! An angel did that!

I want to elaborate on an observation made during the recovery process. I'm seriously left-handed—I would have contorted in any way necessary to use my left hand to grab the rope, especially when adding the fact that my right shoulder had been injured in a basketball accident a few weeks earlier. When I grabbed the rope, it slid through my hand until it hit the knot at the end, then I held on. There is no logical explanation for this: a muscular spasm, a last gasp to stay alive, nothing. However, this was a pivotal moment. I was dead, as the rescuers will certify by their assessments, so this was an unequivocal example of divine intervention.

I believe God, who has used my guardian angel (Psalm 91:11) to save my life several times before, in a graphic fashion, did this. He used my body to grab the rope, and then, later, allowed the rescuers to pry my hand from the rope, demonstrating that he did this, not me.

When my blood pressure suddenly stabilized in the hospital, it was God or a guardian angel who did that, and countless other things in this whole event. To deny supernatural involvement in my story is to overlook obvious interventions that can't be explained by natural means. I have no problem ascribing certain events to the actions of God and his angels because of several other experiences in my life that I can point to. I get goose bumps just thinking about those events, and I shared some of those here as robust evidence for my assertion.

From the conversations I had with those on the other side, it's a wonderful place and infused with pure love. Once there, names are irrelevant—you know them and they know you. Sometimes your soul can require a recognizable physical state, as I experienced with Joanna, and at other times, you can communicate with telepathy. It's a very uncomplicated existence, unfettered by a physical body, at least where I was in heaven. Perhaps there was more, and I would have seen that had I not been sent back. Since there is no time there, it would seem that existence is a continuum.

There are at least six other "near-death" experiences I've had since my Army experience in Vietnam, and each time, He has kept me alive—although shaken and stirred. But this time it was an actual death, and He sent me back. My experience is not about *what* oneness with God is, but that it simply *is*. This is akin to God telling Noah in Exodus 3 that his name is "I Am." He *is*!

I succinctly define faith as belief in something for which you have no physical evidence and no logical proof. One of my friends, Jon

Reelhorn, who owns Belmont Nursery, asked me, "What did that experience—the drowning—do for your faith?"

My immediate answer was, "I have no faith anymore." After I let that sink in for a few seconds, I continued. "I was there on the other side. I felt Him—His presence, His overwhelming love, permeating my very soul. Where we're going is no mystery to me now because I know unequivocally His overwhelming, all-encompassing love. Hence, no need for faith!" He was somewhat shocked at first, but being a brilliant guy, he understood the depth of my answer and smiled—almost laughed. We still smile when we see each other and remember that moment.

While some friends and acquaintances have questioned the validity of my experience in heaven, my sister, Rosemary, was not skeptical when I told her I had seen Joanna. She was glad to be assured that Joanna is fine and as loving as ever, and I could tell she was envious. What mother wouldn't be? Because she has a firm belief in God, she was heartened to know with certainty that someday she'd see Joanna again, and I was glad to confirm it. I told her what Joanna had said to me. "I love you very much and I miss you, but it's not your time to be part of the oneness—you have to go back and love your family!"

"That's what she'd say when she talked to me on the phone," Rosemary said. "She'd say, 'I love you very much,' and she said that every time she talked to you too!" Verily.

I feel like a humbly blessed man who is assured of where I will spend eternity.

Chapter 21
THE NEW ME
Current

Drowning is usually pretty final. In my case, they called it a "near-death experience," but that's not true. I was dead as a doornail when I came out of Bonzai and floated down the river. After my fellow rafters recovered my body and worked tirelessly for twenty-two minutes doing CPR, I was suddenly alive again. One of the most remarkable aspects of my recovery was that most of my personality and intellect remained intact.

A good friend, Dr. Steven Clausen, told me that a surgeon he discussed my case with said my chances of recovery were one in ten thousand, and I would undoubtedly be brain-injured for the rest of my life. But here I am, living an everyday life and definitely in reboot mode! Some aspects of my personality and character have changed. There are several facets of my personality that I, and others, have defined as "altered and even improved."

I used to be quite stoic and firm regarding discipline within my family. My father's attitude was, "Be an example and demonstrate character," and the kids will acquire the traits you want them to focus on. But that's easier said than done. For most of my life before the drowning, I had been critical and harsh with my children when they weren't living up to my standards, which I believed were my father's standards and therefore correct. I was wrong. I was not giving my children a chance to be themselves without a significant dose of my agenda.

While I was recovering, after being in the hospital for almost a month, I had time to reflect on who *the new me* was supposed to be. Because I could feel that I was different, and indeed, I was. My perspective on a lot of things was modified, especially after the therapist helped me unlock the experience "on the other side." Knowing that, I expected to be able to make positive changes in my life that would be beneficial, perhaps even powerful. And they have been. You accomplish a lot more when you have a gentler, kinder, and more considerate attitude towards discipline. People respond much more positively to a guy who's smiling than one who's bellowing criticism and commands.

When we have our grandchildren over for dinner and end up watching a movie on TV, I've found that they all turn and look at me when there's a scene that evokes emotion, whether it's tearing up or something else. Invariably, I'm crying or teary-eyed for most of these scenes, and I quickly notice the kids looking at me. Interesting. They know and sense that I'm overly sensitive and easily affected, sucked in by Hollywood's skill at playing with our emotions, which is unusual for old stoic me. I've become a softy!

I've also changed physically. I've a small collection of cigars that I've accumulated over many years, along with a humidor box to store them in. I've always enjoyed a cigar on special occasions and considered it a special treat. Additionally, a sign of being well-bred was to enjoy a fine cigar. Someone offered me a toke on a fine Cuban cigar, which I was eager to enjoy, but once I'd inhaled it, I immediately broke into paroxysms of choking, almost to the point of throwing up. My tolerances are different now.

The lungs that God had restored in me were not going to be comfortable with activities that He hasn't approved for me—I now assume smoking is anathema to me, which hasn't always been the case.

One interesting consequence of the drowning was an improvement in my golf game. I love to practice at a small nine-hole practice range called Bluff Pointe, located a mile from my house, situated in a flat area next to and level with the San Joaquin River. It's a beautiful place to take a break and unwind. The pro there is Jim Perez, a Christian friend who now owns it, and he's the one who taught me the basics of golf years ago. I went there about a year after getting out of the hospital and saw Jim. "Whoa, here's a dead man walking!" he announced when he saw me coming. I told him the story, which he'd already heard from some of my sons who also enjoy Bluff Pointe. When I got to the "other side" part of the story, he was enthralled and thanked me for sharing. He had no qualms with any of my story.

Then I teed up to hit some balls and used an old three-wood I carried in my bag, which my dad had. It's a right-handed club, though, but I just felt like trying it. Shockingly, I fired it one hundred eighty yards! Right-handed! Remember, I'm left-handed. So I took out my left-handed three-wood and hit it one hundred eighty yards. *Whoa, what's happening*!

Jim was watching this and told me he'd never seen anyone have a "reset" like that, but said, "Hey, go with it!" Over the next two weeks, my right-handed shots became progressively shorter, so I again deferred to my left hand, and things returned to normal. It seemed like my body was recovering some of the traits that I had spent a lifetime acquiring, rebooting to who I used to be. Perhaps drowning was allowing me to change parts of my life, and this was evidence that I should look for these opportunities and embrace them, or at least taste them.

About three years after I got out of the hospital, when I had resumed a normal lifestyle, an old friend from San Jose, Caesar Snee, asked if I'd like to come up to Heavenly at Lake Tahoe and ski for five days. He had a two-bedroom condo there, and ski season was in full swing. I said, "Sure."

"How good a skier are you?" he asked.

"I've been skiing almost every winter since I was twelve," I said, "and although I'm not as good as some of my little brothers, I can hold my own! I wore 'beartraps'—ski bindings that do not break away if you fall—and broke two pairs of woods learning to ski downhill. With these new bindings, it's easy to get crazy, and that's me!"

I waxed my skis, oiled my ski boots, and drove to San Jose, and then to Heavenly in his pickup. It had just snowed, giving us about eight inches of powder, and we were raring to go. The next morning, we put on our skis and caught the little tram to the base of the lift we wanted to take. I was excited because this was the first time I'd ever been to Heavenly, and I hadn't skied in probably eight years. Conditions were perfect. We got on the lift and went up to the top.

I got off the lift okay, but immediately fell. It was like I couldn't balance myself. I got up and went to ski out of the way of people getting off the lift, but I fell again. It was like the first time I'd ever worn skis, or roller skates, or tried to ride a bike.

Caesar waited for me as I tried to recover my balance, but it was no use. The balance that I had spent my youth perfecting and enjoyed so much was gone. I was going to be relegated to the bunny hill until I figured this out. Maybe my old form would return, but I wasn't betting on it. I was so uncomfortable that I gave up after spending the afternoon going back and forth on the bunny hill. All I could figure out was that something had happened to my vestibular control and a memory had been erased.

The same thing that happened with golf was happening with skiing—my body had to learn it all over again. I was beyond embarrassed. However, after reflecting on this embarrassment, I'm not surprised that it happened. My whole life had changed, and subtle aspects of the changes were emerging where I least expected them. Since then, I'm careful not to assume anything. It is indeed a whole new world for me.

On another level, I began to embrace even more the character traits passed down to me. My father, when I was growing up, made it clear to me that "It's important to demonstrate all the points of the Scout law in your daily life—that's real leadership." Scouts must be trustworthy, loyal, helpful, friendly, courteous, kind, obedient, cheerful, thrifty, brave, clean, and reverent. These traits also define much of what the Bible teaches us about what God expects of us and what goodness is. As a Scoutmaster and a Christian, Dad lived that code and passed it on to us Scouts and his family almost effortlessly.

I find it interesting that behavioral exhortations in the Bible align with the way Scouting used to be. I have endeavored to share this attitude with my children, much as he did, and am so very proud of how my children have carried the torch. I'm sure this is part of what God meant when He told me to go back and love my family.

I now have a clearer understanding of the blessing my family has been. After the drowning and during the recovery in the hospital, there was simultaneously a compelling and cathartic experience going on in the waiting room at the hospital, which was a direct extension of the event. Because I had to be comatose on the RotoRest bed for almost three weeks, no one knew whether I was even going to be revived, much less be somewhat the same guy I had been up until now. And then, when they began to withdraw the hypnotics and I became alert, I was intubated and relatively incommunicado, so it was still a "wait and see" posture.

My mother and most of my brothers and sisters were there, as were my children and grandchildren, as well as many friends and acquaintances. Many had to take time off from work to come. As my brother Dwight described in his inscription in the "diary," it was indeed a vigil. This event strengthened our entire family, bringing us closer and fostering a special new sense of respect for who we are, a respect that persists to this day. When we gather for Christmas at the Hellwig's house in Exeter, the home where I grew up and where my sister Rosemary lives with her husband Mark, we relish the time together and the love we all share—more than a hundred of us.

While I have some lung issues and am still dealing with diabetes, I'm happy to say that I'm pretty healthy for a guy who died and came back. I feel very blessed to be alive and living the life God called me to.

I would venture to say that my drowning had a part, although a small part, in being some of the glue that binds us.

Chapter 22
UP CLOSE & PERSONAL
Today

I've changed spiritually. There is no doubt that this experience had a profound spiritual impact on me.

As the events of my drowning, visit to heaven, and recovery unfolded and developed, I assumed an attitude of not just thankfulness and appreciation for God's plan, but genuine joy at being a part of it. It turned out to be a wonderful thing, although we who lived it were stressed to the max. It's a fact of life that the Father never gives us more than we can handle, and that's because He handles it for us, although sometimes we appear to fold under the pressure. We could never handle it on our own, so He is there to lead and guide us toward whatever purpose He has for us. But by keeping our eyes on the Conductor, we can play our part.

"But we know that for those who love Him, for those called in agreement with His purpose, God makes all things work together for good." (Romans 8:28, The Modern Language New Testament, the New Berkeley Edition) I am alive because God has a purpose for me. He told me, through Joanna, it was to "go back and love your family." What does that mean, other than the obvious? I do love my family, and I'm more intentional about it now. But "called" to do so might mean more than that.

One of my close friends had a grandson who drowned. Bill Dietzel was one of my mentors in the American Legion, a retired Air Force master sergeant. He used to walk into a crowded room, whenever we were having an event at American Legion Post 509, and loudly announce, in his deep voice: "I'm Master Sergeant Bill Dietzel, and I'm *proud* to be a Veteran of the United States Air Force." Everything would stop, and Bill would smile, walk around, and shake hands. He was tall and commanded respect just by being there. We loved him and his intense respect for our armed services.

Every year, Bill would orchestrate the events leading up to the Veterans Day Parade on November 11, at 11:00. He made it into a big deal, even getting the Armed Forces Network to broadcast the parade worldwide. With his charisma, bravado, and insight, he turned it into an event the whole city was proud of. On the morning of the parade, which lasted at least five hours, with people lined up along the route, he would wear his dress blues, bloused and shined combat boots, and walk the lineup, making sure everything was in place. He made us proud.

When I was in the ICU and they'd just removed my tubes, Bill came to visit me. He was unusually emotional and told me how special it was that we were friends. He presented me with some wings to wear on my motorcycle vest, issued to graduates of pilot training. "Bill, I can't wear this! I didn't earn it!"

He said, "Bullshit! Wear that with pride. You've been farther in the sky than any of those guys who got them from going to school." I choked back my tears, as did he. I now wear those wings on my American Legion Riders motorcycle vest with special pride.

Several months later, after I'd recovered most of my stamina, he invited my wife and me to dinner at his house. I knew he was constantly entertaining bigwigs at various events, but being at dinner with his family was special. We got seated at the table and enjoyed a special dinner that he and his wonderful wife had prepared. Then he asked me about the other side and wanted to know what drowning was like. I didn't realize until then that he'd lost a grandson to drowning, so this was very hard for him to discuss.

"Bill, I was in the presence of the Creator, and He answered a lot of my questions without me even asking. But I don't have any insight into why things happen, except I can tell you for a fact that God is in charge. He loves us more than we can know, and I felt it when I was there. You've seen what happens in combat, and I know you've witnessed things you can't explain or be proud of, but He covers us and gives us insight. When your grandson was gone, and you felt God had abandoned you, were you angry? I probably would be. But did He give you solace, somehow? Some understanding? Maybe I'm the missing piece in that puzzle, having been in His presence and now back here, telling you that God hears you, feels you, and knows you. And He loves you beyond understanding. And you can bank on it."

"Thank you, Thom. I did need to hear that. But I can't stop thinking about my little guy struggling to breathe and the terror he might have experienced."

"Bill, the second I inhaled the water in the river, I was unconscious. I didn't feel anything—no pain, no anxiety, no dread. I was instantly gone. So I'm betting your grandson, and probably everyone else who drowns, had a similar experience. When you inhale a little water, you immediately cough it up while you're struggling, and the reaction causes you to inhale more! But when you're underwater, you fully inhale it, and that's terminal and drastic, but it's swift and painless."

I could sense that he and his daughter, the mother of the boy who drowned, felt some comfort knowing it was a quick and painless death. To go straight into the arms of God—what a blessing!

A few weeks later, I was at the VA hospital having a blood test for my diabetes, walking down the hallway, and there was Bill, deep in reflection and distressed about something. He immediately perked up when he saw me, but moments later, he shared that he had just learned that he had cancer, and it was terminal. We were blessed to get to visit him for several months after that, and soon he was gone. I felt honored that God allowed me to have at least a small part in his unburdening in his final days. God called me to it.

There was no one of his stature and commitment to take his place in running the Veterans' Day Parade, but it is still carried on much as he designed it, thanks to several influential veterans who have kept it going with respect. Bill's profound love for our military was terrific to see. I'd come to the parade wearing my trench coat and jungle boots, the only part of my old military uniform that still fit, and when he saw me standing in the crowd, he'd stop whatever he was doing, salute me, and come over to hug me. Yes, I miss him.

I feel called to share my story. I have found that when I share the story of heaven with strangers for the first time, there is a universal interest and curiosity. I have come to expect that. But as I continue with specifics, they will either embrace what I'm telling them or go blank. They continue to listen, but it's clear they're experiencing a disconnect. When I see that happening, I realize that the entire experience was intensely personal, from the conversations with my friends on the other side to my observations. In the end, though, there aren't any secrets about what happened—it's entirely my personal experience, and I have no proof. As Arnold used to say on Saturday Night Live, "Hear me now and believe me later."

Let's face it, God has blessed me beyond anything I could have imagined. I am constantly overwhelmed with awe and appreciation for what He has done in my life. All I have to do is relax for a moment and talk to Him to feel His presence. I am overcome with thankfulness for the life He has given me, including the most astounding woman I've ever met and our seven exceptional children, who know and love Him, and now their families, too, with twenty-one of our grandchildren. Sure, there are challenges we're all constantly facing, but that's because this is the world, and we are not of the world! We will always have evil to navigate, but because we have Him in our hearts, we're safe. But this is not our forever home.

Kelly agrees. "One of the things that became very clear to me, and I don't know why it took this accident to do that, is that our life on earth is just the blink of an eye," she says. "The people who have gone before us don't even know they're missing us. So, when I see them again in heaven, our separation will only have been the blink of an eye. I remember an older woman coming into the store, and she had just lost her husband. And I remember the look on her face when she said, 'I just don't know what I'll do.' And I told her that her husband doesn't even know they're separated yet—that he's in heaven and that she's here. I hope she was encouraged because it made me aware of how short our lives are and how the separation from our loved ones is even shorter—the blink of an eye. Whether you die or whether you stay after a traumatic accident like this, it is still a miracle."

When God said through Joanna, "You have to go back and love your family," He wanted me to understand that, among other things, my family would not be the same if I had not lived and couldn't be there as an example. My wife and I both know His love and glorify Him. Kelly and I have modeled our faith for our children, and they have passed it on to their children.

The scriptural admonition to Christians that "All things work together for the good…" becomes graphic when you have had an experience like the one we rafters and our families had that weekend. Because when you are "up close and personal" with a miracle, as I experienced, you can't forget about it and move forward unchanged.

Maybe I'm here to share with others—with you—that it doesn't have to be a dramatic miracle for you to see how He takes our sad and disappointing and even horrific circumstances, and He works them all out in a way that changes us, humbles us, and makes us usable to Him! It's not hard to see His hand at work in our daily lives, but what do we do with that? We share it! It's our testimony. My testimony has given me opportunities to help others.

It's my prayer that this book will be a comfort to you and others. That is why I'm grateful for what happened to me.

Between the moment I breathed river water into my lungs and the split second that I took a breath following CPR, my whole life was forever changed.

It was and is a miracle.

Kelly and I with our children, their spouses, and our grandchildren, at the November 2025 Celebration of Life for Kelly's mom, "Grandma June."

Epilogue

My Heroes

I realize that my family—my heroes and the stars of this book—had their own trauma from my drowning. I knew that they would all be okay, as they are strong and stable people with a lot of faith. But that didn't mean that they didn't have any healing to go through. I spoke with each of them about it, and they shared what it was like for them during the event and what they carried with them afterward. Some of them learned a huge life lesson. Others made changes to their own lives as a result of that experience. All of them had something to say. Here are some of my thoughts about each of them and their takeaways, in order of their birth.

THOMAS: Thomas, being the oldest of my seven children, brown-eyed like his mother, developed into a natural "leader of the pack" quickly. He refined his organizational skills at Central High, where he served as student body president. After graduating, he joined the Army and became an airborne medic. Back in Fresno, he helped open the first Outback Steakhouse in California and later served as a trainer for the company for several years. He is now a restaurateur with three pubs. He is also a successful real estate agent, continuing to work diligently to represent his clients. He's married and the father of two boys.

"I know when I look back," Thomas said to me, "remembering the moment that I realized it was you who was pulled from the water was tough. It was a complete shock to me. But I had no time to waste. I felt I had to start working on you pretty quickly. That was the hardest part. Getting the scene under control. But, ultimately, the results were good. In the end, you've survived, and you're still with us. So I don't know if there's really any PTSD (post-traumatic stress disorder) with me or not because of the positivity at the end. I had to shake off all the rest and say, well, it was a good outcome. Life is good."

TIMOTHY “TIM”: Tim is my number two son. He has always been quick to size up situations, adaptable, and extremely resolute to the point of being hardheaded. He graduated from Fresno State with a degree in information technology and then worked as a real estate agent for several years. Due to his experience with this accident, he went on to become an RN (registered nurse). He met Elizabeth’s future husband, Dr. Joaquin Arambula, while working in the ER at Selma Hospital, for which she is grateful. While raising a family of five children with his wife, Angela, he attended and graduated from San Joaquin College of Law, passed the bar exam, and is now practicing medical malpractice law. His determination and skill are remarkable.

“That trip dramatically changed my life,” Tim said. “Way back, I had finished all my nursing prerequisites at Fresno State and then decided to transfer to business. Then, when you drowned, I spent a lot of time in the ICU with you, also liaising between the medical staff and our family. I remember thinking, ‘This is what I'm supposed to be doing.’ I spoke with a college counselor and immediately entered the nursing program. I finished up in eighteen months. I understood the terminology related to patient care and difficult situations, including saving people's lives. What I take away is that God has a plan. He had us in the right place at the right time to do our best to deal with it. It changed both of us. I've always been pretty laid-back, maybe a little too complacent in my younger years, and this experience lit a fire under me to start being who I'm meant to be.”

PATRICK: Patrick is the third of my seven kids and the first with my hazel eyes. We knew he would be tough when he was small because he was always on the go. As he grew, he became a very thoughtful and caring friend to everyone and an extremely athletic person. He dominated all sports, especially basketball, and was selected for the Valley All-Star East team. At Central High, he was voted Homecoming King for two consecutive years. He played basketball for Fresno State for four years. Among all his teammates, he had the reputation of being able to eat the most pizza. He was usually not the tallest player, standing at 6'7", but his quickness and dominant moves more than made up for his height. Patrick is a successful realtor and a medical device representative. He's the father of twins.

"I felt kind of fearless and invincible when we started out that day," Patrick said. "I never dreamed that we would have any problems. We were all in good shape, and so were you, except for that shoulder, so we'd handle whatever came our way. It was easy until it wasn't. And then I saw you dead. That vision is etched in my mind forever. You looked so bad. I cried and yelled, trying to shake it off, but it was real. When you were revived, I was so relieved, but it took a long time to get rid of that sense of what it felt like to lose you. I'll never be the same. I don't see life as fearlessly as I once did. But I also have more faith and understand resilience better."

NATHAN: My fourth child, Nathan, is known for jumping into problems and riding them out, rather than wasting time worrying about conflicts. At Central High, following in his oldest brother's footsteps, he became student body president. Since he was tall and lanky, he also excelled in basketball. He attended Point Loma Nazarene College, then returned to Fresno after one year, where he played for Fresno Pacific. I was glad to see him move back to Fresno because the drive down to Point Loma, although pretty, was arduous. We always made it a habit to attend as many of his basketball games as possible. After graduation, he attended San Joaquin College of Law in Fresno, passed the bar exam, and is now a successful PI (private investigator) lawyer. Nathan is the father of two.

"I don't think I'm ever doing that again," Nathan said. "Whitewater rafting is not for me. I have some fear of it. I went through it thinking, 'What if one of my kids or someone else I love had to experience what I did?' I know I have some PTSD. However, there were also some productive results. I think it brought our family closer together, Dad, don't you? I didn't die, but you and I experienced something unique that day in the keeper. While I didn't drown, I felt like I was going to, so it held more of a persuasion for life for me. It impacted my mental state for a time, but then there was reinforcement. You were in pretty good shape, actually, excellent shape. You were pretty muscular, you know, going to the gym a lot, and that helped in your recovery. That encouraged me to keep myself fit."

MICHAEL: When brown-eyed Michael was little, the fifth of seven children, we knew he would be tough. He'd run into things, bounce off, and keep going. In high school, he played basketball and volleyball, like all the boys, and also played club volleyball. At six feet eight, he was a beast as a volleyball middle blocker on the Fresno club team, one of the top one hundred in the country. He reminded us of Thor. Pepperdine recruited him with a four-year free ride, but he lost interest after a coaching change and left after the first year. He's always been skilled in math and working with tools, so he became an electrician. And as a father of three, he was prepared for just about any challenges, but not for what was in front of him that day on the Kings.

"I freaked out, totally panicked, until I got to the hospital. I was keenly aware that you could still die, Dad," Michael said, choking up a bit. "And I knew that I needed to pray, so I did. But I had also thought I might drown when we went overboard. Everybody has this fear of drowning, and thinks how scary it is, but after that, I had an entirely different outlook on it. It was peaceful. Once I started to pass out, I wasn't feeling any pain, and I wasn't even panicked anymore. I felt like I was starting to slip away. And I was right there on the verge, but then a wave hit me in the face. It shocked me, and I shook my head, realizing I was okay. But I didn't think you were, Dad. I don't want to feel that way ever again."

ELIZABETH: My daughter is an atypical example of beauty following beauty. Elizabeth has been an exceptional artist since grammar school, creating art across all media—charcoal, watercolor, oil, and photography. Like many artists, she cares deeply about others and endeavors to care for them. Her brothers were protective, making it almost impossible for her to date in high school. Her keen insight enables her to produce highly accurate assessments of situations, making her a valuable member of any team, especially our family. She's smart! I don't think anyone has ever beaten her in Scrabble. (I did once by making up a word—I cheated!) She has always been a joy to be around and has many of her mother's wonderful attributes. She is married and the mother of three girls.

"My brothers were there and saw it all happen. I think because you survived, though, I don't have the trauma like the boys," Elizabeth explained. "But I do have trauma from when my younger cousin, Joanna, died, and I remember everything that happened. It's wild because I was in the car with mom when we got that phone call too. But because you survived, it was not the same. Spiritually, knowing what you experienced confirmed what I've always thought. All the people we love will be with us one day in heaven, just as Joanna is now. I feel very blessed that you are still with us. That was God's plan. I trust Him all the more now."

GREG: As the youngest of seven, Greg always felt he had to be harsher, louder, and reach further than anyone else to get attention—his emotions revealed in his expressive brown eyes. In junior high school, he ran with the kids who seemed to attract trouble and were rebellious, but we knew that wasn't him. One day, he came home with a nose ring! The next day, his mother went out and bought a large fake nose ring, which she wore when she picked him up from school. He was grossed out; that was the last of the nose ring! But at least he was in school. I will always be amazed at his strength, fortitude, and incredible endurance on the hikes we've been on. Indeed, as he matured, he became an excellent Christian and father of three girls. Greg has been managing a successful sports grill for many years.

"It just made me realize that family is important, and I needed to be a better person because you never know when your time is up," Greg said. "God's real, you know? I think the one question people go through life wondering is how to prove God is real. But right there on the river, my question was answered. God showed himself that day. For me to get that question answered was comforting. So, I think if anything, it just made me a better person. I'm so glad I can cherish time with people now because we never know when it's their last day. My wife always says, 'Don't let a tragedy be the reason why you celebrate somebody you know—celebrate them while they're alive.'"

GORDIE: Number nine of my siblings in our family of ten offspring, and being shorter than everyone else, Gordie should be considered an overachiever. He was a student body president at Exeter Union High School, a cross-country runner with impressive times, and a swimmer. Gordie's amazing dives from the two-meter board and the ten-meter platform rival some of what you see in the Olympics. He finished third in the Valley in the last meet he competed in. Gordie had four kids but lost one. Our kids were all very close—my Greg and his Jeremy, and his twins, Michaela and Seth, hung out with my Elizabeth and Michael. I've always had a special appreciation for him.

"Brain damage can happen pretty quickly, so we liked to tease you, Thom, that you had a brain injury." Gordie laughed. "But the truth is, you're a miracle. The main miracle that day was the helicopter's ability to land precisely where it was needed. I recall speaking with the pilots; they believed this was a body recovery, not a rescue. Kelly told us how serious it was and that the outcome would have been different if the water hadn't been so cold. Our brother, Larry, a respiratory therapist, said that the cold water made a significant difference in your lungs. With him there, we had a guy in the dugout who helped calm us. It's all a miracle. It reminded me of the movie *Abyss,* where the Ed Harris character goes underwater and starts breathing water. I thought maybe, scientifically, if it's enriched in some way, your body, blood, and lungs could adjust. But knowing that your lungs were full of water for a long time, and you still survived—that's a miracle."

KELLY: Last, but certainly not least, I don't know what would have happened to me if I hadn't had Kelly in my life. She also had to deal with all my daredevilish behavior and near-death experiences, but she was always level-headed and did what needed to be done.

When I returned home from Vietnam in 1968, I enrolled at College of the Sequoias (COS) in Visalia and shared an apartment with another veteran from Exeter, who grew up just a block from my house. I was a stickler for a clean kitchen and neat rooms, and James "Moss" Britten thought I was pretty bossy. His girlfriend, Norma Chamberlin, decided I needed to meet her big sister, Kelly, whom she considered extremely bossy. One afternoon, I was sitting on our couch watching TV with my then-girlfriend when Norma came in with her sister, Kelly. They were giggling as they walked into the bedroom and still giggling when they sauntered by us on the way out.

Kelly grew up in Weiser, Idaho, and moved to Visalia for her first year in high school in 1965. She told her mother that she wouldn't marry until she was over thirty and probably wouldn't have kids. Promises, promises! She had one older brother and two younger sisters, which earned her the "bossy" moniker.

Unable to get blond-haired, brown-eyed Kelly out of my mind, a week later, I called her, and she agreed to a date. All five feet eight of her looked lovely when I picked her up for our first date. It was on my birthday, and I took her to dinner with my family in Exeter. When I reached over to buckle her seatbelt for the fifteen-minute drive, I got my first kiss! My whole family was waiting in the dining room when we got there—six brothers and two sisters, and we had a great dinner. Six months later, we were married.

I changed majors to optometry and was accepted into the Los Angeles College of Optometry (LACO)—now Southern College of Optometry—and we moved to an apartment in Inglewood. LACO was located next to USC (University of Southern California), making it an easy commute. Our first baby was scheduled to be born in August 1972, and we decided to give birth naturally, using Lamaze. Still, when the doctor told me I'd be excused from the delivery room if there were any issues, we decided on a homebirth. We found a doctor who would come to our apartment for the delivery, and it went so well that we decided that any more children would be born that way. I couldn't see how I could support a family while attending school, so

I dropped out and got a job. Eventually, all seven of our children were born at home, with Kelly directing the cast!

As our family grew, Kelly perfected tremendous skills in organizing activities and planning. Getting the boys to basketball and volleyball practices at rural Central High in Fresno required a fourteen-mile round-trip drive, often three times a day. Complicated schedules and activities, plus working and lots of other duties like feeding all of us, would have frazzled anyone but the strongest of warriors, which she epitomized. Additionally, she is a realtor—her father, Jack Chamberlin, owned Westland Realty, and her youngest sister, Jennifer, owns the Keller Williams Realty franchise in Fresno—and she quickly became skilled in this field.

In 1995, Jack purchased Bullard Uniforms, which had stores in Santa Barbara and Dublin, from a client who had won the lottery. As a result, Kelly and I became the managers and eventually owners since we had a proven track record of working well together.

I believe that I couldn't have found a better woman to spend my life with and raise a large brood with. And when I drowned, she took charge, in typical Kelly fashion, and kept us going when I couldn't. I'm forever grateful to her and for her.

Thom and Kelly

About the Authors

Without a doubt, Thom Miller has led an exciting life. He has accomplished many things throughout his nearly seven decades, both in his business endeavors and in his personal pursuits. Those who know him do not expect that to change.

Growing up in the rural agrarian town of Exeter, California, Thom was the oldest of ten children. Acquiescing to his mother's desire that he excel in English and math, Thom attended Bellarmine Prep High School in San Jose, a school with stringent standards. His four years of studying Latin haven't hindered his natural literary flair, as he asserts that Latin is the foundation of the English language.

Thom's father was the local optometrist, a career Thom had considered following. But after earning an AA with a focus on pre-med, he decided it wasn't the best path for him. A year after graduation, he enlisted in the Army and went to Vietnam.

Returning to Exeter, Thom quickly found the love of his life, Kelly, and the two married. Fifty-five years later, they enjoy their seven children and twenty-one grandchildren. He feels that God has blessed him beyond measure.

Thom has been quite the entrepreneur, having started several businesses, including an insulation installation company, which employed many people. However, the medical uniform store in Fresno that he and Kelly ran for over thirty years gave him a sense of accomplishment. Interestingly, aside from a writing course he took, he says he learned a lot while writing material for his businesses and communicating with his employees.

In Thom's new book, *Between Two Breaths*, Thom shares how God has often stepped into his life, sometimes in dramatic fashion. But the last time God intervened was most life-changing, hence the book. “I didn't plan to write a memoir,” Thom says. “I'm a private person. But this story isn't just mine—it's about something bigger.”

Retired now, Thom and Kelly are happily living their golden years in Fresno, California, in their beautiful home on a cliff overlooking a scenic river. He finds it a great spot to write.

A longtime lover of words, literature, and the process in between, it's no coincidence that Valeri Mills Barnes has become a prolific editor and book-writing coach.

Valeri mastered a wide range of skills throughout her twenty-year career in publishing. She jumped into the deep end of the industry when she purchased a regional weekly newspaper in California. For thirteen years, she coordinated all aspects of the popular newspaper, including writing, editing, formatting, and publishing. She also expanded to produce two successful national trade magazines.

Throughout that time, she ran a freelance business editing books of all types and coaching authors through their writing process. She discovered that it was her true joy, especially working with the authors, and continues to freelance today.

In addition to her own business, Valeri is a contracted Senior Editor at a publishing house in L.A., where she wears many hats—adding ghostwriting to her skill set—and works with clients across the United States and internationally.

Valeri resides in the Central Valley of California, where she enjoys being near her children and grandchildren. When not working, she's visiting her family, teaching a Bible study, enjoying wine tastings with friends, or fleshing out her latest book idea with other authors.

Note From the Publisher

BERRY POWELL PRESS
Carmen Berry, Founder
New York Times Bestselling author

We at Berry Powell Press are committed to cultivating authors and their life-changing messages through a collaborative, creative community. As such, we are delighted to publish *Between Two Breaths* by Thomas Miller with Valeri Mills Barnes. There are many ways this book aligns with our vision and purpose.

First, it is the way the book is written. While it is a memoir of Thom's unique story, the literary approach is innovative, incorporating the perspectives of many who shared in Thom's gripping journey. I felt as if I was in the raft beside them, splashed by the frigid waters and tossed by the rapids of the Kings River. The thrill, the panic, the desperation, and ultimately the power of love and family are palpable. It is a book you will remember long after the last page.

Secondly, the story is not only engaging but also life-inspiring. The spiritual threads are not forced or preachy; they are authentic and ring true. The determination of Thom's family to fight for his life long after others had given up hope demonstrates that love has more power than we often realize.

Finally, Thom's experience of facing death resonates with everyone as we must all, at some point, confront our own mortality. However, the unique insights he gained through his personal journey offer a sense of hope and courage in life's most challenging moments.

This story is about an ordinary family, albeit a large one with seven children, who seem unique in their experiences. But Thom's gift is his awareness of the hand of providence in his life. While we may not be as in tune with the spiritual presence in our lives, Thom's story can remind us that we are all God's children.

www.ingramcontent.com/pod-product-compliance
Lightning Source LLC
LaVergne TN
LVHW010657110826
845149LV00014B/3135

* 9 7 8 1 9 5 7 3 2 1 2 6 4 *